An Exorcist Explains
How to Heal the Possessed

FR. PAOLO CARLIN

An Exorcist

EXPLAINS

How to Heal
the Possessed

And Help Souls
Suffering Spiritual Crises

Translated by
Charlotte J. Fasi

SOPHIA INSTITUTE PRESS
Manchester, New Hampshire

Sophia Institute Press
Box 5284, Manchester, NH 03108
1-800-888-9344

www.SophiaInstitute.com

Sophia Institute Press® is a registered trademark of Sophia Institute.

Library of Congress Cataloging-in-Publication Data

Names: Carlin, Paolo, author.
Title: An exorcist explains how to heal the possessed and help souls suffering spiritual crises / by Fr. Paolo Carlin ; translated by Charlotte J. Fasi.
Other titles: De cura obsessis. English
Description: Manchester, New Hampshire : Sophia Institute Press, 2018. | Includes bibliographical references.
Identifiers: LCCN 2018003447 | ISBN 9781622825202 (pbk. : alk. paper)
Subjects: LCSH: Demonology. | Exorcism. | Spiritual warfare. | Catholic Church—Doctrines.
Classification: LCC BX2340 .C3713 2018 | DDC 235/.4—dc23 LC record available at https://lccn.loc.gov/2018003447

First printing

To the honor and glory of God;
To my father and mother;
And to the holy archangels,
Michael, Raphael, and Gabriel.

We beg you God, through the intercession and the
help of the archangels Michael, Raphael, and Gabriel,
for the deliverance of our brothers and sisters
who are enslaved by the Evil One.

Contents

Part 4
Discerning and Accompanying

Appendices

Preface

What a useful book!

What a valuable aid for priests, educators, parents, and anyone desiring help with problems caused by the Devil, understanding his existence, and recognizing his action!

Within these pages we find *a catechism on the mission of Jesus Christ,* who came to liberate us from the power of the Evil One, to establish the Kingdom of God, and to bring us to full communion with Him and with one another.

The author makes an *excursus from Sacred Scripture to the Church's Magisterium,*[1] showing readers how Jesus and His Church are aware of Satan's presence and of how he tempts man to do evil.

In a detailed analysis the author describes how the action of the Evil One takes shape in the life of a person. Then he points out the means necessary to combat him and turn him away.

For priests and for families of those who have spiritual problems, but without claiming to have exhausted all practical suggestions, the author gives concrete examples showing how to accompany and help the afflicted.

His language is clear, direct, and precise, unencumbered by roundabout expressions. At times, readers may feel a little

---

[1] The teaching authority of the Church.

annoyed, especially those who have never had experience with exorcisms or have never been in contact with loved ones who have been tormented by the Evil One.

Some readers may even think that some assertions here are exaggerated, but those who have had these experiences will not have any difficulty recognizing the truth and objectivity of what Fr. Carlin describes.

This is also a useful book *for those who know nothing about the Devil, vexations, obsessions, and possessions.* In it we have a guide that helps us to keep the door closed to Satan, to make life choices according to God's law, and to be extremely prudent and clever before the subtle tempter.

In particular, the text shows that there are *persons, places, practices, and philosophies that must be avoided* in order not to compromise our spiritual and human life.

In all, the author helps us to understand *how to live our earthly life in health and serenity* and to reach the eternal life that Jesus promised.

Readers of this book will come to understand how important it is for all of us to live a life of faith in Christ, listening to Him in the Gospel, dialoguing with Him and with Mary and the saints in prayer, and meeting Him in the sacraments and in participation in the ecclesial life.

Giuseppe Verrucchi
Archbishop Emeritus
Ravenna–Cervia

Act of Consecration to Mary

Mary,
Mother of Christ and of the Church,
we consecrate ourselves to you,
and we entrust to you our lives,
our families and our work.
O Mother, give to your sons and daughters
that inexhaustible capacity to love
that bursts from the pierced side of the Crucified One.
Mary, luminous morning Star,
placed by God on the horizon of humanity,
extend your mantle over us,
pilgrims on the paths of time
among multiple risks and snares,
and come to our aid
now and at the hour of our death. Amen.

—*St. John Paul II*

An Exorcist Explains
How to Heal the Possessed

Introduction

In this century that bridges two millennia, we find ourselves living in an obviously satanic culture and a modernity tied to hypertransgressions, nihilism, materialism, and the occult. Today the Devil is gradually losing his fearful bearing and becoming an ally of those who desire magical power or illusory knowledge, which used to be eclipsed by faith in the only God and His Church.

Satanism is the extreme form of transgression and rebellion; it is the pursuit of magical powers and control over others and over one's own evolution. Many adolescents, left to themselves, are wearing the five-pointed star, the cross turned upside down, and the number 666 (the name of the beast). They use drugs; surround themselves with obscure, deadly symbols; play games that evoke demons; and listen to music that extols dissolution, violence, and the powers of darkness.

There is no longer a distinction between good and evil. Everything is looked for in man, and power is sought in the gods. Many cling to beliefs in the magical hidden powers that were practiced in the Renaissance and to the occultism of the 1600s and 1700s. One synthesis worked out by Freemasonry describes man's aspiration to become like God through secret initiations and ceremonies that seek to recover man's "omnipotence" in the Garden of Eden before the Fall.

Occultism is a network of intercommunicating sects and groups. A person accepted by many of these groups can practice a kind of esoteric nomadism. Added to these is the philosophy and practice of esoteric oriental beliefs, which center and divinize man in the universe, giving him control over energies that go beyond his nature.[2]

Our day is marked by a broad diffusion of openly superstitious or deviant cultural practices. The lack, in many persons, of an incisive faith experience and solid religious convictions, the loss of some important Christian values, and the obscuring of the profound meaning of life create a climate of uncertainty and precariousness, which in turn favors recourse to forms of divination and at times extremely aberrant rites, such as those of the cult of Satan.

We must emphasize that, contrary to popular belief, these aberrations occur not only where culture is lacking, but even where there is a high level of culture and education.

From pastoral experience one observes that today superstition and magic live together with scientific and technological progress. This is not surprising, considering that science and technology are not able to answer the ultimate questions of existence: not competent about the ends, they deal only with the means.

---

[2] An example is the philosophy and practice of yoga with its tension toward ecstasy, like that of reaching a Nirvana, with its negation of human suffering through the avoidance of everything fundamental. In reality, suffering is an important element in coming to know oneself and one's human nature. Also, reiki, the prana therapy (spiritual healing), and acupuncture can operate on the energy of the body with disciplines, rituals, and manipulations.

Introduction

Scientific and technological efficiency instill in man the illusory conviction of being self-sufficient and immortal. Superstitious and magical practices enhance their value by acquiring an aura of scientific credibility, claiming roots in medicine, psychology, psychiatry, and information technology. Furthermore, there are, in support of magic, entrepreneurial businesses of vast dimensions with conspicuous financial backing.

Against this reality, this book aims to furnish some useful references and criteria to help the reader to recognize the Evil One's immense, variegated sea of tricks and provide some instruments of defense and liberation from his concealed attacks or manifestations in our lives.

Part 1

The Evil One: "The Mystery of Iniquity"

In the current cultural climate there is a diffuse interest in the occult and the satanic, to which the social media contributes, supporting and echoing it. On the other hand, broad sectors of contemporary culture underestimate or even deny the action of Satan both in history and in individual lives. Often, they borrow from the allegorical and poetic language of Scripture and popular preaching, and from Tradition in attempts to refute, without the necessary discernment, the true content of revelation and the teachings of the Church.

The key announcement of Jesus Christ is the coming and the nearness of the Kingdom of God. Expulsion of demons is a manifestation of the Kingdom of God. "If it is by the Spirit of God that I cast out demons, then the kingdom of God has come upon you" (Matt. 12:28).

The Devil's best trick is that of persuading man that he does not exist. Because original sin has tainted human nature in its image and likeness of God, we commit evil effortlessly. Goodness, which before sin was natural to man, who remained in total communion with his Creator, is now only the result of commitment, vigilance, and combat.

Let us begin with some observations concerning the rebellious Angel. First, we must clarify whether we have the correct essentialistic, ontological concept of Satan as a spiritual person or merely a relational, psychological concept of him as an intellectual idea. We must, moreover, allow for the complexity of phenomena that can be attributed to various causes, including disturbances caused by mental illnesses, paranormal psychological conditions, moral disorders (sins), and obsessions.

We must find the balance between attributing every evil to Satan, seeing him everywhere, and totally denying his existence. Therefore, for all that regards Satan, his nature, and his existence, we shall examine biblical revelation and what Jesus Himself says of this fallen angel.

1

What Sacred Scripture Teaches

The Nature and Existence of the Devil

In spite of the criticisms and denials of some philosophies and theologies, the existence of the Devil is a fact revealed in Sacred Scripture.

Evil that exists in the world finds its cause in man's choices and their origin in Satan. The mystery of evil (*mysterium iniquitatis*) comes from the Angel's ill use of his creaturely liberty and from his rebellion against the Creator.

The Devil is a creature, a pure spirit, an angel, not united to a body. His nature as a creature was good from the moment he was created by God. As a spirit gifted with intelligence, will, and liberty, he is a person.

But after his rebellion against God, he was defeated ontologically. This is his situation. With his actions, he denies his bond with God, his being a creature created by God and of the same spiritual nature, claiming it arrogantly as his own. He is a person, a creature, but with a spiritual nature.

From a comprehensive reading of Sacred Scripture and traditions even more ancient, we learn that evil did not begin with man, but with a rebellious angel who, preceding his fall, was called *Lucifer*, a Latin term meaning "bearer of light." Lucifer was tasked with transmitting to man the light, the truth, and the knowledge of God, and of cooperating with God and man in the conservation and development of the beauty and harmony of the universe.

This angel, however, exalted with the splendor and greatness God gave him, rebelled, and with the excuse of assuming his place in the governance of creation, claimed for himself adoration owed solely to God.

By refusing God's plan, Lucifer dragged down with him one-third of the angels of Heaven (see Rev. 12:4). Frequently during exorcisms, the motives emerge for his fall and the fall of the angels who followed him. Even today, while we celebrate the ministry of liberation, which the Church has entrusted to us, we exorcists hear demons protest with hatred and anger toward God, because He made Himself a man in Christ, assuming our human nature, which they consider inferior to their angelic nature. Likewise, they do not accept that His Mother, Mary, although created, like every human creature, of spirit and matter, soul and body, has been elevated by God above the angels, who are spirits without matter. They scorn matter, valuing it as something low and inferior.

In God's plan, it is the Word, which takes flesh and is made man, that gives consistency and meaning to the entire universe, including the angels. In refusing God's loving plan for all creation, Lucifer and a portion of the angels caused its devastation, introducing evil, suffering, and death, which in the original creation did not exist.[3]

---

[3] One cannot attribute to God the source of evil in the world, nor can He be considered the "cause" of evil; rather, He is the creative cause of being free. The origin of evil is rooted in the limitation on liberty, both angels and men: it, being finite, is exposed to failure, as St. Augustine and St. Thomas observe.

Because of this, even from the beginnings of creation, God established that the Incarnation of the Word would also be redemptive, with the objective of saving human creatures. Therefore,

---

In order to impede evil, God would have had to create beings deprived of liberty, but this would have denied them the capacity to do good with awareness. Liberty, however, demands the possibility of choosing good and also the Supreme Good, which is God.

If we consider our human experience, we must recognize that each affective, authentic tie cannot be founded on compulsion: love is true if it comes from a free choice. God, who is Love, in order to attain the love of His creatures, exposes Himself to the risk of their senseless refusal. Precisely because He is Love, God cannot establish—either toward the angels or toward men—relationships of mastery and subjection. The willingness to love unites angelic and human creatures to God, bringing them to eternal happiness. God created us free in order to give us the possibility of opening ourselves to His love, enabling us thereby to participate in His divine nature, resulting in eternal beatitude. If He had created angels and men without liberty, they would have been incapable of loving and therefore incapable of attaining the goal of their existence, which is perfect love in the happiness of the Beatific Vision of the Triune God.

Regarding liberty, a correct, holy use or a reprobate abuse is possible. God is not able to force us to use it positively or to exclude the possibility that we will use it poorly. The disorder consists in the dramatic choice of angels and men, impugning their own liberty in order to oppose God, refusing His love or the love of other creatures. This choice of opposing God directs angels and men toward eternal perdition. Therefore, through liberty, we either freely save ourselves or we freely lose ourselves. Thus, God, although wishing the eternal beatitude for all His creatures, had also to make possible their eternal perdition. He did not predestine anyone to Hell. It is the creature himself who freely chooses a state of perdition. See F. Bamonte, *Gli angeli ribelli* (Paoline Editoriale Libri, 2008), pp. 31–32.

while He was creating, God was already thinking of His Son
made man (Jesus Christ) as Redeemer, and of His Mother, as the
collaborator with the Redeemer Son.

The Old Testament and the Devil

The Hebrew noun *satan* has many meanings: in the martial sphere
it indicates the "adversary" (see 1 Sam. 29:4), in the juridical "the
opposer who bars the way" (see Num. 22:32), in general "the bad
counselor" (see 2 Sam. 19:22). This last meaning is reflected again
in Matthew 16:23 and Mark 8:33.

Hereafter, the substantive became a proper noun, *the* Adversary, *the* Accuser (1 Chron. 21:1), and designates a spiritual
being that implacably sets men against God (Zech. 3:1–2; see
Job1:6ff.; 2:1) and is their principal adversary, counseling them
to sin (1 Chron. 21:1).

In the Old Testament, we find few texts that speak of the
Devil. The primary intention of the authors of sacred writings is
to speak of God, the Lord of creation and history. The Seventy
(LXX),[4] in translating the Old Testament, used the word *daemon*
(demons). In Zechariah, Satan is at the right of the Angel of
the Lord in order to accuse the high priest Joshua. Satan wants
God to do justice, but the Angel of the Lord defends Joshua,
who is asking for mercy (cf. Zech. 3:1–5). In the book of Job, the

---

[4] The first translators of the Bible from Hebrew to Greek were
called the Seventy. (Probably the number was rounded off for
the conventional use of the abbreviation LXX. Actually, there
were seventy-two. According to the *Letter of Aristea*, at the request of King Ptolemy II Philadelphus (285–247 B.C.), seventy-
two sages (scholars) came from Jerusalem to Alexandria, Egypt,
to translate the Torah (Jewish Law) — that is, the five books of
the Pentateuch — from the original Hebrew to Greek.

action of Satan is controlled by God (Job 1:6–12; 2:1–7) when Satan wishes to put Job in a situation of disobedience. In the first book of Chronicles, Satan appears as the one who wishes to convince the king to make a census of the people, an act of arrogance toward God (1 Chron. 21:1–7). The book of Wisdom affirms that death entered the world because of the Devil's envy (Wisd. 2:24). Chapter 3 of the book of the prophet Tobit informs us that the demon Asmodeus, the envious and evil spirit, attacks the husbands of Sarah (Tob. 3:8). Asmodeus is conquered by the prayers of Sarah and Tobias and by the help of the archangel Raphael. In the book of Leviticus, Azazel is the demon to whom is offered the scapegoat for the rite of expiation (Lev. 16:8, 10, 26), and in the book of the prophet Isaiah, Lilith is the feminine demon that inhabits the ruins (see Isa. 34:14). The Elilim, bad spirits (the "nothing") are opposed to Elohim (the gods). These last representations clearly reflect the religious influence of Israel's neighbors; nevertheless, no dualism or confusion is seen in the Israelite faith.

Jesus and Satan

In the New Testament the chief adversary is identified with the Devil (1 Pet. 5:8: "your adversary the Devil") and with the "great dragon and ancient serpent" that was expelled from Heaven, took refuge on earth (Luke 10:18; Rev. 12:9; 20:2), tempted Jesus Christ (Matt. 4:1–10), and is still tempting man (Acts 5:3; 1 Cor. 7:5; 2 Cor. 11:14; 12:7) and producing physical illnesses in man (Luke 13:16). Satan, moreover, has his own kingdom (Matt. 12:26; Mark 3:23ff.), which is in open warfare with the kingdom of Christ (Luke 22:31; 1 Thess. 2:18; 2 Thess. 2:9; Rev. 2:9–13; 3:9) and also spreads clever and false doctrines (Rev. 2:24). Judas, Christ's betrayer (Luke 22:3, John 13:11), and other followers of

Christ (1 Tim. 5:15) become Satan's prey. At the end, Satan will be crushed by Christ's faithful (Rom. 16:20). When thousands of years have passed, Satan will be temporarily liberated from his prison and will seduce many nations, including Gog and Magog, and he will fight the last battle against the City of God, but he will be defeated and wiped out forever (Rev. 20:7–10).

There is a considerable amount of information regarding demons in the New Testament. Much of it is derived from titles attributed to Satan: the liar; the Devil, the one that divides; Beelzebub, the lord of the flies; Belial, the enemy. Other terms used are: the unclean spirit, the Evil One, the great dragon, the ancient serpent, the Antichrist, the prince of this world, the armed strong man, the father of lies, and the murderer from the beginning.

There is little information about the nature or description of the Devil, and nothing is said about what form he has. Rather, he is presented as the one who sows discord, who wishes to distance Christ and His disciples from their mission. His power is superior to men's, and he does not fear placing snares before Christ or Peter. His actions can be physical (causing illnesses) or moral (inducing sin), but his power is totally subject to Christ.

Jesus came to destroy the works of the Devil (1 John 3:8) and to reduce to slavery the lord of death (Heb. 2:14). Jesus is the "stronger one"; He has conquered the evil sovereignties and ruling forces (Col. 2:15), and He has the power to judge the Devil (John 16:11).

The Gospels announce the great and joyous event of God becoming man, who has taken the name Jesus (Joshua: "God saves") and who has wrought our redemption in order to liberate humanity from the power of Satan and from sin. Satan succeeds by binding men to him through temptation that is unresisted, becoming sin and an offense to God.

During the years of His public life, Jesus frequently chased demons from the bodies of the possessed. The Gospels include descriptions of Jesus' exorcisms and the conferral of power and the mandate that He entrusted to the Church to expel demons in His name.

Jesus Himself reveals the significance and fundamental importance of the exorcisms when He says: "If it is by the finger of God that I cast out demons, then the kingdom of God has come upon you" (Luke 11:20). With these words, Jesus affirms that His expulsion of demons is the sign of the coming of the Kingdom of God among men and of His mercy (Matt. 12:28), which men could once again accept, unlike the demons, who definitively refused Him.

In the New Testament, there are numerous passages that relate the exorcistic activity of Jesus and His struggle against the Evil One:

- Mark 1:32–34, 39: "That evening, at sundown, they brought to him all who were sick or possessed with demons. And the whole city was gathered together about the door. And he healed many who were sick with various diseases, and cast out many demons; and he would not permit the demons to speak, because they knew him. And he went throughout all Galilee, preaching in their synagogues and casting out demons."
- Matt. 4:23–24: "He went about all Galilee, teaching in their synagogues and preaching the gospel of the kingdom and healing every disease and every infirmity among the people. So his fame spread throughout all Syria, and they brought him all the sick, those afflicted with various diseases and pains, demoniacs, epileptics, and paralytics, and he healed them."

• Luke 7:21: "In that hour [Jesus] cured many of diseases and plagues and evil spirits, and on many that were blind he bestowed sight."

• Luke 8:1–2: "And the twelve were with him, and also some women who had been healed of evil spirits and infirmities: Mary, called Magdalene, from whom seven demons had gone out."

• Luke 13:32: "Behold, I cast out demons and perform cures today and tomorrow, and the third day I finish my course."

• Acts 10:38: "[Jesus] went about doing good and healing all that were oppressed by the devil, for God was with him."

Jesus works these miracles as a sign of His power against the kingdom of Satan and as a partial realization of the Kingdom of God, which will be completed in a perfect way in the eschatological epoch with the Second Coming of Christ.

In the Gospels, there are several detailed descriptions of exorcisms:

• the demoniac of Capernaum: Luke 4:31–37; Mark 1:21–28

• the blind and mute demoniac: Matt. 12:22–23; Luke 11:14

• the Gerasene demoniac: Matt. 8:28–34; Mark 5:1–10; Luke 8:28–34; Luke 8:26–39

• the mute demoniac: Matt. 9:32–34

• the daughter of the Canaanite woman: Mark 7:24–30; Matt. 15:21–28

• the young epileptic demoniac: Mark 9:14–19; Matt. 17:14–20; Luke 9:37–44

• the crippled woman: Luke 13:10–17

The Gospel of Mark begins with an exorcism (Mark 1:21–28). In this miracle we see a pattern:

1. The demon manifests himself in the possessed person.
2. Jesus threatens and commands it to go out of the person, thus pointing out the violent and cruel nature of the demon.
3. The demon leaves.

Jesus commands demons in the same way as God. Although His formulas are brief, the demons obey without resistance. At times, when it concerns cures, their obedience is immediate and instantaneous. Sometimes the demons confess the identity of Christ, "the Holy One of God" (Mark 1:24; Luke 4:34).

Jesus does not do extraordinary things. It is only His word that makes the demons go out of the obsessed, and He gives this power to His disciples: "He called to him the twelve ... and gave them authority over the unclean spirits.... So they went out and preached that men should repent. And they cast out many demons, and anointed with oil many that were sick and healed them" (Mark 6:7, 12–13).

When these seventy-two, who cast out demons, returned, Jesus said to them: "I watched Satan fall like lightning from heaven. Look, I have given you power to tread down serpents and scorpions.... Do not rejoice that the spirits submit to you; rejoice instead that your names are written in heaven" (Luke 10:17–20).

Expelling demons is a sign that identifies the disciples: "In my name they will cast out demons" (Mark 16:17). It does not involve magical acts: it requires faith and the practice of virtue. Faith in Jesus, prayer, and an orderly life are the indispensable conditions for the efficacy and success of the cures (Mark 9:28–29).

In the Acts of the Apostles, the exorcistic activity is done in the name of Jesus: "I charge you in the name of Jesus Christ to come out of her" (Acts 16:18). Christ's work is carried out by the apostles Philip (Acts 8:6–7) and Paul (Acts 16:18; 19:12). Jesus sends Paul to convert those who are under the power of Satan (see Acts 26:17–18). After Pentecost the disciples can cure persons tormented by unclean spirits (Acts 5:16). Such is the activity of Philip (Acts 8:7). Paul also works uncommon wonders: through handkerchiefs and aprons that had contact with him, many were cured of their illnesses and the "evil spirits came out of them" (Acts 19:11–12).

Expulsion of demons is one of the characteristics of the Kingdom, and it is tied to faith. When it is done by the disciples, it is done in the name of Jesus (Mark 16:17; Luke 10:17).

In St. Paul's letters, the word *Satan* appears a good ten times. St. Paul tells us that struggle against the Devil is difficult:

> For we are not contending against flesh and blood, but against the principalities, against the powers, against the world rulers of this present darkness, against the spiritual hosts of wickedness in the heavenly places. Stand therefore, having girded your loins with truth, and having put on the breastplate of righteousness, and having shod your feet with the equipment of the gospel of peace; above all taking the shield of faith, with which you can quench all the flaming darts of the evil one. (Eph. 6:12–16)

The mystery of iniquity is at work in the world (see 2 Thess. 2:7). In the struggle against evil, in order to combat the wicked man, the son of perdition, the Evil One, the Adversary, the one who assails all that bears the name of God, proclaiming himself a god (see 2 Thess. 3:1–3), it is necessary to have the grace of Christ.

The coming of Satan will be manifested with every type of trick, but St. Paul does not speak of the Devil; rather he speaks of Christ, who conquered him with His death and Resurrection. Powers, principalities, dominions, angelic powers, and thrones are submissive to Jesus Christ, the Risen One (see 1 Cor. 15:24; Gal. 8:38; Col. 1:16; 2:3–20; Eph. 1:21; 2:2).

The book of Revelation depicts the grand struggle against the Evil One. Satan is the name of the enemy who appears more frequently than the others. He relies on allied powers, but nothing can succeed against the slaughtered Lamb, to which God has subjected everything. Revelation tells of the great victory of Christ over Satan and encourages Christians on the basis of this certainty.

In the same book, the great struggle between the dragon and the woman (who symbolizes Mary and the Church) describes the battle with the Devil in which Mary and the Church are victorious. Even if, as time passes, the drama seems to increase in intensity, Satan knows the battle is lost: victory is in the hands of Christ.

In the Gospels, we discover how Jesus' temptations (Matt. 4:1–11; Mark 1:12–13; Luke 4:1–13) and His miracles and wonders are an anticipation of His victory over Satan. In fact, the subject of the temptations is the messianic concept of Christ, which is contrary to that of the satanic. In this context Christ affirms the power of the divine Word over the demon.

Jesus' battles with the forces of evil and His expulsion of demons from the obsessed are called a sign of the coming of Christ: "If it is by the finger of God that I cast out demons, then the kingdom of God has come upon you" (Luke 11:20).

The dramatic struggle between Jesus and Satan gradually increases as it approaches the Passion, but "the gates of the underworld can never prevail" (see Matt. 16:18). One of the most significant components of Jesus' ministry appears in the Gospel of St. Mark, which presents the expulsion of the demons as true battle scenes. Jesus has power (*dynamis, exusia*)[5] over Satan, who falls before Him like lightning from Heaven (cf. Luke 10:18). God's action and His power over the forces of evil are in the form of exorcisms. We read indirect allusions to exorcisms in Matthew 8:16, Mark 1:32–34, and Luke 4:40–41.

We find true exorcisms, where clear awareness of Christ is manifested, in Mark 1:21–28, Mark 5:1–20, Mark 7:24–30, and Mark 9:14–29. The time for God's salvific action against the demon has arrived.

The demon observes the re-creation of the human person through the presence of Christ and the action of God. In casting out demons, Jesus does not use the Judaic ritual, only the strength of His power: Jesus "went about doing good and healing all that were oppressed by the devil" (Acts 10:38). What is extraordinary is that, through Jesus, God calls man to collaborate in the struggle against the Devil. Jesus gives this power to the apostles (Mark 6:7) and the same is manifested in the early Church (Acts 8:7; 19:12–16).

In the parables, Jesus speaks of Satan as a personal spiritual being, not as an absence of goodness or the personification of evil. In Luke 11:22 He calls him the strong man; in Matthew 13:18–23, in the explanation of the parable of the sower, Satan, identified with the birds, takes away the seeded word; in Matthew 13:24–30, in the parable of the weeds, Satan sows evil in the hearts of men.

---

[5] *Dynamis*—the transforming power that inhabits the Word of God; *exusia*—authority used in the sense of moral influence.

Jesus also reveals this life's battle when He teaches us to pray the Our Father. The last of the seven petitions offered to God is against Satan: *apò tou porenú,* "liberate us from the Evil One." If it were liberate us from *any evil,* the expression would be *apò touto porenú,* "liberate us from this evil," or "liberate us from every evil."

In fact, the New Testament uses the word *porenú* twelve times for the Evil One, the Devil. For Christ, combating the Evil One is the mission of His entire earthly existence. In the Passion and death of Christ, Satan is present: in the hour of darkness, Satan enters into the heart of Judas (Luke 22:53; 22:3). Death is the work of the Devil (Wisd. 2:24), and Christ accepts it out of love (John 10:18; see Heb. 2:14–15). The Passion of Jesus Christ in obedience to the Father is a judgment against the prince of this world (Phil. 2:7).

In the New Testament, through the life of Jesus and His action, we have four fundamental teachings of the Christian faith.

1. The victory of Christ over Satan, which is opposed, in a thousand ways, to his assault upon the Kingdom.
2. Evil is ascribable not only to the human will but also to the fruit of diabolical action.
3. Satan is a personal, spiritual being, but he is not omnipotent. Man perceives him in a confused way.
4. With the coming of Christ, a terrible struggle was begun between Christ and Satan. Satan won in a definitive way, but this struggle is protracted until the end of history. Concerning this, he still has a certain power over man (see the book of Revelation).

In conclusion, we can say that:

1. Through events, Sacred Scripture presents notions that we cannot express with concepts, and nearly always

uses a highly imaginative and symbolic language that hides while it reveals (think of the *Leviathan*).

2. In His person and His action, Jesus Christ has a central theological role in human history. Salvation is attained through faith in Him and through participation in the grace that comes to us in His Spirit.

3. Even though we are still enduring the hard struggle of good over evil, recognition of Christ's victory is already substantially demonstrated in the watershed event of His death and Resurrection.

4. Because, as Genesis 3 teaches, evil does not originate solely from man's will, it cannot be overcome solely with human powers: that requires the major involvement of divine grace.

5. Man's free will is the determining factor in the net distinction between the voluntary sins of man and the satanic action of possession.

6. Because man alone cannot fight an angelic being who is more powerful than he is, man has need of God for his existence and salvation.[6]

---

[6] See John 12:31; 16:11; Gen. 3:15; Rev. 4:20 and also 1 Chron. 21:1; 2 Sam. 24:1; 1 Thess. 2:18; 2 Thess. 2:11; Matt. 4:5–11; 16:23; Luke 22:3; 8:26–39; Mark 9:29.

2

What the Church Affirms

Tradition and the Fathers of the Church

Some Doctors of the Church hold that Lucifer ("bearer of light"), wishing to be at the center of the universe and considering our human nature inferior to his angelic nature, did not accept God's plan of assuming human nature for himself. Moreover, he did not accept the fact that the woman from whom God would be born as a true man, would be elevated above all creatures, human and angelic, thus becoming the queen of men and angels.

Theologians maintain that, in God's plan, Lucifer, the first angel, committed a sin of pride, rebelling against God. So how was it possible that he could commit a sin, given his perfection? Because God alone is sinless (impeccable), therefore all creatures can sin. If it were possible for a creature not to sin, then that would be a gift from God, not a natural condition.[7]

According to the Fathers of the Church the angelic sin can assume various natures:

- *The sin of lust*: We find this in the book of Enoch, in Origin, and in St. Irenaeus. For Clement of Alexandria, it consists in a sexual union between the decadent angels and the daughters of men.

---

[7] See St. Thomas Aquinas, *Summa Theologica*, I, Q. 63, art. 1.

- *The sin of pride*: the desire to be like God and also that the Word assume not a human nature, but an angelic one.
- *The sin of arrogance*: the wish to arrive at supernatural perfection solely through one's own powers. As a result, the fallen angels did not survive the trial of faith that required submission to the will of God.

Like every sin, the angels' sin has personal consequences: above all, they were deprived of the supernatural goal and, therefore, the Beatific Vision. Although their natural intelligence and their natural gifts, in general, remained unchanged, they lost their supernatural knowledge. Therefore, the knowledge of the fallen angels is inferior to that of the good angels. In particular, their knowledge is dark: what they know they cannot relate to God. Moreover, since their choice is definitive, their will remains persistently evil and their sin irreversible for all eternity. Whereas, in relation to God, human liberty is flexible before and after the choice, the angelic will is flexible only before the choice.[8]

According to *The Shepherd of Hermas*, there exists the way of light and the way of darkness. In the *Letter of Barnabas* appear the terms the Agitator, the Bad One, the Black, and the Lawless. In the *Martyrdom of Polycarp* (bishop of Smyrna), we find the Envious and the Jealous. According to Papias of Hierapolis, Satan is the leader of the angels in charge of the movement of the cosmos.

For the apologetic Fathers, the demons are not the gods of paganism. Other Fathers affirm that the demons are the children of marriage between the angels and the daughters of men. (According to St. Irenaeus of Lyons, Satan was jealous of the first man.

---

[8] See *Catechism of the Catholic Church* (CCC), nos. 391–395.

For Origen, the gods of the pagans are demons. They have an invisible body, are heterosexual, and require nourishment. Lucifer, their leader, is an apostate and the prince of this world. He and his angels rule men who allow it.

Among the Cappadocian Fathers, Basil affirms that the angels were created good, but they became bad. According to Gregory of Nyssa, Satan is an angel who is jealous of man and one day will be conquered.

St. Augustine affirms that the angels were created good in view of the harmony of the universe. Those who rebelled against God sinned in the first instant of their creation. But the action of Satan is restrained by Christ. The Devil, the Antichrist, is a king who persecutes the Church. According to St. Augustine, Hell is eternal.

Other Fathers and writers are Cassian, who says that each man has a bad angel; Gregory the Great, who affirms that the Christian is in a continuous struggle against the demon; Caesarius of Arles, who describes the works of the devil; and St. Anselm, whose *On the Fall of the Devil* says that the good angel fell irrevocably of his own accord (*propria voluntate*), without involvement by God. This is the sin of pride and envy. When Satan sinned, he fell into chaos.

St. Bernard's demonology conforms to what the Bible says. St. Thomas Aquinas in *De demonibus, de malo* affirms that demons do not have a body and that their sin consists in having desired a supernatural life and glory that is independent of God. Such a sin of arrogance was committed after their creation. They cannot go back, and they cannot know the future, but, through secondary causes—that is, by studying the choices made by men—they can predict the future. Furthermore, their knowledge is not tied to charity.

The Popes

In view of the mandate given by Jesus, the high pontiffs have always spoken of the Church's struggle against the forces of the Evil One (see Luke 10:9; Mark 16:18; John 12:31–32; Rev. 12:9).

In citing some of these popes, we recall Leo XIII, who composed the prayer to St. Michael the Archangel as protector of the universal Church; and Paul VI who, in a general audience on November 15, 1972, affirmed:

> In the case of the Devil, evil is not merely an absence of something but an active force—a living, spiritual being who is perverted and perverts others. This is a terrible reality, mysterious and frightening. The refusal to acknowledge the Devil's existence is a departure from the picture provided by biblical Church teaching. So are the claims that he is a self-sustaining principal who, unlike other creatures, does not owe his origin to God, and that he is a pseudo-reality, a conceptual, fanciful personification of the unknown causes of our misfortunes. The Devil is our number one enemy, our preeminent tempter. We know that this dark, disturbing being exists and that he is still at work with his treacherous cunning; he is the hidden enemy who sows errors and misfortunes in human history.

St. John Paul II, in more than one encyclical, also spoke of the Devil, affirming that announcement of the Kingdom of God is always a victory over him.[9] Consequently, building the Kingdom is always exposed to the entrapments of the Evil One.

---

[9] "I saw Satan fall like lightning from heaven" (Luke 10:18).

Struggle against evil is the Church's struggle until the last days of salvation. The pope exhorted us neither to distort nor to deny the power of Satan. With respect to human creatures, demons are angels, personal, powerful spiritual beings who have radically and irrevocably refused God and His Kingdom.

Satan seeks to lead man to live with an attitude of competition, insubordination, and opposition to a relationship with God, the Creator. In fact, Satan's sin consists in refusing God, known to the light of intelligence and revelation as the Infinite Good, subsisting in love and holiness.

St. John Paul II points out how this fallen angel, the father of lies, has, to a certain extent, conquered the human realm, and as a result of the sin of man's progenitors, is the destroyer of supernatural life. The dominance and influence of Satan embraces the entire world. His action consists in tempting men to evil and in influencing their imagination and their superior faculties: their intelligence and their free will, in order to turn them in a direction contrary to God's law.

The introduction to the *Rite of Exorcism* states that, in certain cases, the Evil Spirit exercises his influence not only on material things, but also on the body of man, which we speak of as diabolical possessions.

At Casa Marta, October 30, 2014, Pope Francis, at the beginning of his ministry, commented on a passage of the Letter of St. Paul to the Ephesians:

> In this generation, like so many others, people have been led to believe that the devil is a myth, a symbol, an idea, the idea of evil. But the devil exists, and we must fight against him. He is a real presence who acts while hidden even if one is skeptical or only mildly convinced.

Borrowing from St. Paul, the pope urges us to clothe ourselves with the armor of God, the truth. Then he describes Satan with these precise terms:

> The devil is a liar, the father of lies; and in order to fight him we must have truth on our side. He is a sower of discord and incites arguments that lead to serious errors. The Devil does not toss flowers at us; rather, in order to kill us, he shoots burning arrows. We need to put on the shield of faith, the helmet of salvation, and the sword of the Spirit that is the Word of God.

According to Pope Francis, the antidote rests with faith and with the awareness that life is a battle:

> The Christian life is a battle, a beautiful battle, because when God emerges victorious in every step of our life, this gives us joy and great happiness: the joy that the Lord is the victor within us, with his free gift of salvation. But we are all a bit lazy in this battle and we allow ourselves to get carried away by our passions, by various temptations. That's because we are sinners, all of us! But do not get discouraged. Have courage and strength because the Lord is with us.

The Christian life is a continuous battle against temptations, the demon, the world, and the passions of the flesh. The Devil exists, and it is necessary to defeat him. "The Word of God tells us this," the pope affirms, "and it requires strength and courage to resist and to proclaim it." Later the Pontiff says: "In order to go forward in the spiritual life, one must struggle. It is not a simple clash; no, it is a continuous battle." Pope Francis also reminds us that the enemies of the Christian life are the Devil, the world, and the flesh (the passions, which are the wounds of original sin). He observes that the salvation Jesus gives us is gratis, but we are called to defend it:

> From whom do I have to defend myself? What must I do? Paul tells us to put on "God's full armor," meaning that God acts as a defense, helping us to resist Satan's temptations. Is this clear? No spiritual life, no Christian life is possible without putting on God's armor, which gives us strength and protects us.

The Authoritative Teachings of the Catholic Church

From her first official pronouncements, the Church has spoken of her enemy entrapping men. In 325, the Nicene Creed of the Council of Nicaea spoke of Christ's descent into Hell. In 381, the Council of Constantinople condemned unauthorized exorcisms and a false cult of the angels. In 745, the official text of the Synod of Rome mentioned demons; and in 1215, the Lateran Council IV proclaimed the following theological definition of the faith:

> We firmly believe and confess without reservation that there is only one true God, eternal, infinite, and unchangeable, incomprehensible, almighty, and ineffable, the Father, the Son, and the Holy Spirit.... They are the same substance and fully equal, equally almighty, and equally eternal. They are the one principal of the universe, creator of all things, visible and invisible, spiritual and corporeal, which by almighty power from the beginning of time made at once out of nothing both orders of creatures, the spiritual and the corporeal, the angelic and the earthly, and then the human creature,

who, being composed of spirit and body, shares in both orders. The devil and the other demons were, in fact, created naturally good by God, but they became evil by their own doing. As for man, he sinned at the suggestion of the devil's power.[10]

In 1547, the Council of Trent declared that because of Adam's sin, men fell under the power of the Devil: "*Sub potestate diabolic ac mortis.*"[11] Therefore, "Christians must struggle against the demon."[12] Summarizing the doctrine of St. Paul, the same Council of Trent affirmed that man, a sinner, "is under the power of the Devil and of death."[13] In saving us, God "has delivered us from the dominion of darkness and transferred us to the kingdom of his beloved Son,[14] in whom we have redemption, the forgiveness of sins" (Col. 1:13–14).[14] To commit sin after Baptism is to "abandon oneself to the power of the demon."[15] This, indeed, is the early and universal Faith of the Church, attested to from the first centuries in the liturgy of Christian initiation, when catechumens, on the point of being baptized, renounce Satan and profess their faith in the most Holy Trinity and in Christ, their Savior. For this reason, Vatican Council II, being more interested in the contemporary Church than in the doctrine of creation, warned the faithful to be on guard against the activity of Satan and the demons. Like the Councils of Florence and Trent, this

---

[10] Heinrich Denzinger, *Enchiridion Symbolorum* (San Francisco: Ignatius Press, 2012), 800.

[11] Ibid., 1521.

[12] Ibid., 1541.

[13] Ibid., 1521.

[14] Ibid., 1523.

[15] Ibid., 1668.

Council also affirmed with St. Paul that Christ liberates us from the power of darkness (see Col. 1:13).[16]

Summarizing Sacred Scripture, the Council's document *Gaudium et Spes* (the Pastoral Constitution on the Church in the Modern World) says that "the whole of human history has been a hard combat against the powers of evil, stretching, as our Lord tells us, from the very dawn of history until the last day."[17] Elsewhere, Vatican Council II renews the warnings of the letter to the Ephesians to "put on the whole armor of God, that you may be able to stand against the wiles of the devil" (Eph. 6:11).[18] That's because, as the same Constitution reminds us, "we are not contending against flesh and blood, but against the principalities, against the powers, against the world rulers of this present darkness, against the spiritual hosts of wickedness" (Eph. 6:12).[19] It is not surprising, then, to observe that the same Council, wishing to present the Church as the Kingdom of God, as it was from the beginning, invokes the miracles of Jesus and to this end also calls attention to His exorcisms.[20] It is on such occasions, in fact, that Jesus said: "… then the Kingdom of God has come upon you" (Luke 11:20; Matt. 12:28).

The Council did not wish to propose new dogmatic definitions about the Devil. It spoke of him through his action in the

---

[16] See Vatican Council II, Decree on the missionary activity of the Church *Ad Gentes*, nos. 3 and 14, in Austin Flannery, O.P., ed., *Vatican Council II: Constitutions, Decrees, Declarations* (Collegeville, MN: Liturgical Press, 2014).

[17] Vatican Council II, Pastoral Constitution on the Church in the Modern World *Gaudium et Spes* (GS), no. 37b, in Flannery, *Vatican Council II*.

[18] See also Dogmatic Constitution on the Church *Lumen Gentium* (LG), no. 48d, in Flannery, *Vatican II*.

[19] See also *LG* 35a.

[20] See *LG* 5a.

world and the actions of the Church opposing him in order to fulfill the mission given to her by Christ, her founder. Vatican Council II clearly believes in the personal existence of demons. Its discourse about them is somber and its doctrine biblical.[21] It emphasizes Christ's final victory, the victory that has been working throughout history and will be complete at the end of it. The redemption worked by Christ has not yet borne all its fruits because, in order for it to be effective, we also must be involved.

The *Catechism of the Catholic Church*

The Church participates in the victory of Christ over the Devil. She exercises this victorious power through faith in Christ and prayer that in certain cases can assume the form of exorcisms. History continuously submits to the influx of the rebellious spirits (Eph. 2:2), and little by little, as it approaches its end, the devil is becoming more violent; but the definitive triumph will be Christ's.

The *Catechism of the Catholic Church* (CCC) affirms that the existence of these immaterial, spiritual beings (called angels by Sacred Scripture) is a truth of faith. Sacred Scripture is as

---

[21] LG 13: Men have been deceived by the Devil. LG 17: The Church confounds the devil. LG 35: The conversion implicates a battle against the sovereigns of the kingdom of darkness. LG 48: Man must put on the armor of God that we may be able to stand against the wiles of the Devil and resist the Devil. GS 2: Christ breaks the stranglehold of the Evil One (cf. GS 22; AG 3). GS 13: Man is tempted by the Evil One. Christ has come to throw out the prince of this world. SC 6: Christ has freed us from the power of darkness. AG 9: Christ overthrows the rule of the Devil.

clear as the unanimity of Tradition (CCC 328). Behind the disobedient voice of our first parents lurked a seductive voice, opposed to God, which out of envy made them fall into death (CCC 391).

In this being, Scripture and Church Tradition see a fallen angel, called Satan or the Devil (John 8:44; Rev. 12:9), who in the beginning was a good angel created by God. Scripture speaks then of a sin of the angels, which resulted in a condition of permanent opposition to God without the possibility of reconsideration. Their sin is different from the sins of men, not because of its nature (every sin is alienation from God), but for its inability to be forgiven, its spiritual and eternal irrevocability. This is because of the angel's nature as a pure and definitive spirit. As a spirit, an angel adheres irremovably to its choice, which, because of its completely spiritual nature, it cannot change. The angelic nature is such that, through one act alone, it decided for itself irrevocably.

Human nature, on the other hand, is not capable, through solely one act, to arrive at absolute goodness or irrevocable perversion, but has need of many acts. Although the sin of the first human couple was very serious, it was not an irremediable evil. Therefore, in original sin there are some mitigating factors:

1. The progenitors were seduced. That is, there was a tempter who deceived them.
2. As human beings composed of soul and body, they were not capable of a radical choice and irreparable evil.

The sin committed by the first parents was serious and painfully consequential; however, it allowed them — and all other men who would follow them — the possibility of conversion and repentance.

We know that such a possibility is not feasible after death.[22] The afterlife is the continuation of our life on earth in the sense that with death there is no break or alteration in the continuity. The difference is in the altered condition in which we shall find ourselves: even at the final resurrection we shall be without the body. If on earth we went toward God, we shall continue to go toward Him after death until we reach Him. Like the tree that bends, we fall in the direction in which we were inclining. So shall it be with our will: it will remain freely but immutably oriented. As it was oriented in our life, so shall it be received at our death.

At the moment of his death, the man who on earth always lived in search of God and in obedience to Him will go to Paradise. If in life he went toward God but at the moment of death was not yet ready to see God's face because of imperfections from which he was not yet liberated, he shall submit to a period of purification in Purgatory, which is capable of rendering him acceptable to enter Paradise. Finally, if a man, because of an obstinate attachment to his sin, closed himself off from God's light and from His merciful love even at the moment of death, he will find himself in the eternal perdition of Hell.

God's judgment does nothing other than act on what man himself has decided. Therefore, we must not think of God's judgment of Hell as His retaliation for man's transgression. This is not the case: the relationship between sin and Hell is an intrinsic connection. Hell is not a punishment that God inflicts on us;

---

[22] "It is the *irrevocable* character of their choice, and not a defect in the infinite divine mercy, that makes the angels' sin unforgivable. 'There is no repentance for the angels after their fall, just as there is no repentance for men after death'" (CCC 393; St. John Damascene, *De Fide orth.* 2, 4: PG 94,877).

rather it is an evil that we ourselves wish: it is the complete and definitive attainment of what man wished and continues to wish. He will—paradoxically—be contented, because he will attain forever what he wished: he wished for sin, and he will languish forever in his sin.

In the episode of the pleasure-seeking rich man and the poor man Lazarus, we hear Abraham say to the rich man who is in Hell: "Between us and you a great chasm has been fixed, in order that those who would pass from here to you may not be able, and none may cross from there to us" (Luke 16:26). This abyss refers to the impossibility of changing destinations after death: he who is in Hell will never be able to pass into Purgatory or Heaven, and he who is in Purgatory or in Paradise will not be able to go to Hell.

Sin consists in refusing God and His Kingdom through one's free choice (CCC 392), incited by Satan's deceitful seduction: "You will be like God" (Gen. 3:5). As Sacred Scripture affirms, the Devil is a sinner from the beginning (1 John 3:8) and the father of lies (John 8:44). The gravest of his mendacious works is inducing man to disobey God. Sacred Scripture attests to the wicked influence of the murderer, the tempter of Jesus, from the very beginning.

The *Compendium of the Catechism of the Catholic Church* succinctly explains this angelic metamorphosis: "Angels, created good by God,... were transformed into evil because with a free and irrevocable choice they rejected God and his Kingdom, thus giving rise to the existence of hell" (no. 74).

From his origin as the bearer of light, Lucifer became darkness. At that moment he became Satan. The *Catechism of the Catholic Church* defines Satan as "the Evil One, the angel who opposes God, the Devil (from the Greek, *dia-bolos* which means 'the one who has gone astray'), the one who wishes to obstruct God's plan and the work of salvation accomplished by Christ" (see CCC 2851).

The *Compendium of the Catechism of the Catholic Church* describes the end of Satan's actions and the demons after their fall: "They try to associate human beings with their revolt against God" (no. 74). Satan and the other rebellious angels work in the world in the midst of men, inciting them to join their rebellion against God; they want men to join them in their refusal to recognize Him as the true God.

The goal of satanic action in the world and toward man is absolutely unique: Satan wishes to drag men to Hell. He does not wish man to participate in eternal beatitude. Out of envy he opposes the work of salvation, seeking to persuade him to persevere in the pseudo-truth of "do what you want! You are your own God!"

The Devil continuously reproposes to man a distortion of the principles of good and evil that God has dictated. God alone knows what is true and good; and out of love, He proposes it in the commandments. St. John Paul II wrote in the encyclical *Veritatis Splendor*: "God's law does not reduce, much less do away with, human freedom; rather it protects and promotes that freedom."[23]

Satan, on the other hand, tries to influence man to establish his own version of good and evil. The Devil continuously instills in man the lie that he will be happy and fulfilled solely if he is independent from God. In reality, he tosses man into a horrendous abyss of sin, destruction, and death.

[23] John Paul II, encyclical *Veritatis Splendor* (August 6, 1993), no. 35.

An important aspect in the mystical experience of St. Faustina Kowalska involves the action of the Devil. She puts us on our guard against Satan, who seeks to convince us that Hell does not exist, trying in every way to distract us from perceiving the real possibility of damnation that lurks behind a life marked by irresponsible choices, opposed to love of God and neighbor.[24]

We must emphasize that the power of Satan is not infinite. He is a powerful creature because he is a pure spirit, but he is still only a creature, and he cannot ultimately impede the building of the Kingdom of God, nor can he seize man: he can only tempt him.

The action of Satan causes serious spiritual harm and also, at times, physical harm, but this action is permitted by Divine Providence. That Divine Providence should permit such diabolical activity is a great mystery but we know that God works with those who love Him (see CCC 395; Rom. 8:28).

Jesus rejects the temptations of the Devil, and the Devil leaves him until a later time (Luke 4:13). Jesus is the victor over the Devil, and His victory anticipates His Passion, when He conquers the tempter for us (see CCC 538–540). Through his death, Jesus, the author of life, reduces to impotence the one who had the power of death: the Devil (Heb. 2:14; see CCC 635).

The *Catechism* teaches that Baptism is liberation from the Devil. Therefore, during its celebration one or more exorcisms are pronounced (no. 1237); with His Passion, Christ liberated us from Satan and from sin (no. 1708); each form of worship of the cult of Satan, divination or magic, goes against the first

---

[24] See St. Maria Faustina Kowalska: *Divine Mercy in My Soul* (Rome: Libreria Editrice Vaticana, 2014), p. 199.

commandment (nos. 2114–2117); the lie is diabolical (no. 2482); through the devil's envy death entered the world (no. 2538).

The Lord's Prayer offers seven petitions to the heavenly Father. In analyzing the seventh, "deliver us from evil," evil is not an abstraction; rather, it clearly indicates a spiritual person: Satan, the Evil One, the angel who is opposed to God (CCC 2851–2854).

Christ Himself asked the Father to liberate the disciples from the Evil One, who seduces all the earth and brought sin and death into the world (John 17:15). When Satan is definitively defeated, creation will be liberated from the corruption of sin and death. In fact, the world lies under the power of the Evil One, but the Evil One does not touch those who are born of God, and those who trust in God do not fear the Devil (1 John 5:18–19; St. Ambrose).

On the Cross, Christ conquered the Devil definitively. As a result, the prince of this world has been judged and expelled from Paradise. After falling to the earth, he confronted the woman, but he did not seize her, says the book of Revelation (Rev. 12:4–6). When we pray for liberation from the Evil One, we pray also for liberation from all the evil he promotes in the world.

3

The Evil One and Today's Society

In his first letter, St. John writes: The whole world is in the power of the Evil One" (1 John 5:19). The presence of the Evil One strives little by little to have man and society distance themselves from God. The shrewdness of Satan in the world is that of leading men to deny his existence in the name of reason. Yet the power of Satan is not infinite. He is only a creature, powerful to the extent that he is a pure spirit, but always a creature, limited and subordinated to the will and dominion of God. The power of Satan cannot annul the power of God; and Christ conquers the prince of this world. Christ made Himself participate in our human nature even to the Cross in order to reduce to impotence, through death, the one who has the power of death, the Devil: "The reason the Son of God appeared was to destroy the works of the devil" (1 John 3:8).

In our daily life we encounter and live in a culture that is no longer oriented to universal, infallible criteria, insofar as reference to God is denied by many sectors. God must be understood as an infallible spiritual being, omnipotent, omniscient, and omnipresent, who, according to our Christian faith, is incarnated in the person of Jesus, with whom men may have an interpersonal relationship. This explanation is necessary, since in Eastern philosophies God is understood as a primordial energy of which man is a part, which suggests a way for the discovery of such energies in himself.

We define culture and today's way of thinking as *satanic*, as in the Hebrew word *satan*. The Hebrew noun *śāṭān* is a derivation of the root s ṭ n, which means being hostile, opposing and assailing, even if only morally, and also defaming and slandering.

Our current society can also be defined as *diabolical* (from the late Latin *diabŏlus*) a word that was adopted from the Greek for contradictor or opposer, in order to translate the Hebrew *śāṭān*.

Today's way of thinking and acting characterizes a culture that is mendacious, divisive, and confused. A resulting systemic conflict that has replaced the building up of absolute values is obvious to everyone. Economic progress and the advancement of technologies have increased, notwithstanding uncertainty for the future and isolation caused by a growing individualism. This creates disorder, anxiety, and even panic, which result in a spasmodic search for answers and the means by which to attain well-being and fulfillment, but guided solely by one's own thought. Having refused the standards and values of traditional culture, many seek them elsewhere, particularly in Eastern cultures and philosophies.

The *Dhammapada,* one of the fundamental texts of the more ancient Buddhist tradition, opens with these verses:

> The mind precedes all mental states,
> they are all mind wrought.
> If with an impure mind a person speaks or acts,
> suffering follows him,
> like the wheel that follows the foot of an ox.

> The mind precedes all mental states;
> if with a pure mind a person speaks or acts,
> happiness follows him
> like his never-departing shadow.[25]

Succeeding to live with a "pure mind" is the ultimate goal of the existentialist Buddhist ethic. It understands the mind to be like a mirror: egotistical and individualistic thoughts are stains and incrustations on it that cloud whatever image is reflected. A mind free from impurities is free from the burden of suffering. Meditation, discipline, and interior work correspond in metaphorical terms to the cleansing of the mirror.

In philosophical terms, it seeks recovery of the original condition of the soul, which precedes each intellectual judgment — an idea not foreign to current Western mystics, but decisively counter to the path taken up by Western philosophy. Christianity, in particular, accepts various particular references that exist outside the person and that can be discovered solely through an existential ethic that is part of a personal relationship with God. Such a relationship is defined by the guidelines that are God's Commandments.

Christian altruism — the search for a connection to God and neighbor — stands opposed to Buddhist egocentrism. The latter specifically excludes personal relationships. Indeed, the overall objective of Buddhism is the annulment of the distinction between the subject knower and the object known.

In the course of history, it has been established that the mind of man is capable of two types of knowledge: the first is rational, held in great esteem by the West; the second is

[25] *Dhammapada*, 1–2.

intuitive, which, in general, is exactly the opposite of rational knowledge and in keeping with the attitude of the East. Rational knowledge belongs to the field of science and to the intellect, whose function is that of analyzing, comparing and contrasting, measuring and categorizing. It is a system of abstract concepts and symbols. In this way, it encounters the world as if that world were constituted by separate parts and constructs an intellectual map of reality in which things are reduced to their contours.

Eastern philosophy has a concept of the world in which the two fundamental themes are the unity and interdependency of all phenomena. It considers man an integral part of this system. What interests Eastern philosophy is the search for a direct experience of reality that transcends not only intellectual thought but also sensory perception.

Buddhists call knowledge derived from an experience of this type "absolute knowledge." It is, they say, a direct experience of absolute essence, undifferentiated, undivided, and undetermined (unspecified). Absolute knowledge is, then, a nonintellectual experience of the totality of reality, an experience that begins from an unusual state of awareness that can be called meditative. It is the reality of the life of the Self that lives solely as it is; the bare experience of life (that is lived only now).

In this way, according to Buddhism, consciousness becomes unlimited, infinite. It is cosmic consciousness (universality is the intrinsic nature of the mind). The unconscious that is beyond the sphere of scientific research can only be felt: it is necessary to learn to master the unknown wisdom of the Self. At that moment, however, when consciousness turns inward and begins to know itself—at that moment in which it becomes the object of its own knowledge — illumination flourishes.

When these principles are considered by someone from Western culture, they are seen as self-exultation, egocentrism, and the divinization of man as a created being.

In claiming that consciousness can become infinite, Eastern philosophy is false and misleading about the truth of being and about creation itself. That is, it becomes a way to interfere with relational reality by promoting contact with the "I" that is enclosed in introversion and egocentrism. In this way it becomes satanic and diabolical, mendacious in regard to the relational anthropological reality of man; and it produces division through a specific individualism and egocentrism.

St. Paul writes to Timothy:

> I charge you in the presence of God and of Christ Jesus who is to judge the living and the dead, and by his appearing and his kingdom: preach the word, be urgent in season and out of season, convince, rebuke, and exhort, be unfailing in patience and in teaching. For the time is coming when people will not endure sound teaching, but having itching ears they will accumulate for themselves teachers to suit their own likings, and will turn away from listening to the truth and wander into myths. As for you, always be steady, endure suffering, do the work of an evangelist, fulfil your ministry. (2 Tim. 4:1–5)

What St. Paul pointed out precisely describes today's world. We witness the phenomenon of individualism founded on a do-it-yourself formation of the human personality, which refuses any reference to the other, any standard other than one's own will and one's own feelings.

Teachers are sought who highlight and exalt personal qualities, to transform subjective criteria into absolute objective criteria and standards for life choices. Such teachers, for the sake of financial gain or because of their various philosophies, preach the realization of full humanity by anthropocentric terms or by divinization.

In this way, they infiltrate all the habits and behaviors popular in today's world. By means of these ideas, even a simple act of making progress in one's own work, in itself a legitimate aspiration, can become a sphere of choices and behaviors that annihilate the aspirations of others, without even respecting their existence.

Also, they try to extend the centrality of personal feelings beyond the limits of human nature. We witness today the progressive self-affirmation inherent in gender ideology, wherein gender is considered a matter of free choice. In fact, a new anthropology is being affirmed based on annulment of the sexes and an exaltation of the criteria of personal choice. Also, in the economic and social field we see a gradual transformation of the equilibrium and realities that until today have guided human progress. We see, in fact, how personal profit has become the preponderant criterion with respect to the common good.

Part 2

The Evil One's Objective: To Destroy Man

The malicious action of the enemy toward creation, and in particular against man, is based on envy and jealousy of human nature. Lucifer, the Angel of Light, was the first of the angels put in charge of creation. His own name led him to commit the sin of arrogance and to rebel against God. Lucifer's task of naming the plants and animals passed therefore to man, a creature inferior to the angels, who are pure spirits.

After the corruption of human nature that incited man to disobey, God chose to recreate man in His image and likeness, assuming for Himself man's human nature. Through Jesus, the Son, God incarnated, He worked a new creation. All this aggravated the hatred of the Evil One for man and for God. The Devil, because of his disobedience, was expelled from Paradise, thrown upon the earth, and, having rightfully earned these torments, was banished from God's presence.

In the temptation described in the book of Genesis, we find a lie. Evil is presented under the appearance of good, so God's commandment appears as a limitation of man's free choice. In this way, disobedience to God came to be seen as a good. After having been seduced into disobedience by the Devil, man experiences a profound disillusionment with himself and discovers his nakedness.

But not every temptation comes from the Devil. St. James, in his letter, affirms: "Each person is tempted when he is lured and enticed by his own desire" (James 1:14); and the Devil can profit from the occasion by augmenting the power of the temptation. God has given men prayer as a weapon to conquer temptations, as long as they have Jesus, the Lord and Savior, as their center.[26]

The extraordinary action of the devil, his most conspicuous and sensational manifestation, occurs most often after temptation has succeeded in putting a person on the path of disobedience toward God, which is sin.

In the case of persons in a state of grace and in communion with God—and in some saints—extraordinary action by the devil is permitted by God. In these cases, our Lady first asks that the person attacked accept this trial. One of these cases involved Annalise Michel (Emily Rose, in the film that bears her name), whose cause for beatification is now open. Others involved St. Gemma Galgani and St. Pio of Pietrelcina.

There is also a steady increase in the phenomenon of persons—both the faithful and atheists—who live with sufferings for which medical doctors cannot find solutions or precise clinical cures. These people speak of having received spells or curses (the evil eye) or of having observed strange happenings in their house or on their persons. Some, when in the presence of people they encounter or at certain places, speak of feeling profound interior sensations or disturbances, such as confusion, fear, or anxiety.

Others think that all magical practices are reducible to a popular credulity without any foundation. Certainly, there exists magic that is solely fraud and is operated by charlatans who swindle and

[26] *Code of Canon Law* (CDC), no. 2849.

create tricks that are contrary to God's commandments. We must, however, emphasize that not every exercise of occult practices is solely a trick or a harmless belief deprived of foundation. To participate in the world of the occult or personally to practice or exploit other peoples' experiences regarding rituals tied to the occult and esoterism, or both, can cause damage both to the psychophysical life and the moral and spiritual life. In extreme cases, such damage can add to the effects of the extraordinary diabolical phenomena of obsession, vexation, possession, and infestation. Those who exercise the ministry of exorcism have verified that these cases often have their origin in occult practices.

Therefore, in discerning the extraordinary action of the Devil, priests must find out in the first interview if there have been any occult experiences on the part of persons seeking help from the exorcist.

What sense must we give to the occult evils that people say they are experiencing? Does it concern people who are psychologically weak?

Three types of people can be distinguished. There are:

1. Persons who are ill with psychological or psychiatric problems. These persons need either a psychologist or psychiatrist, not an exorcist, since usually they are expressing physically their own problems or are identifying the cause of their illness with the person of the Devil.

2. Persons who are mentally healthy but with disturbances and physical illnesses of a diabolical origin, who wind up with various levels of possession. These persons need solely a priest exorcist.

3. Persons with physical and psychic illnesses that are indistinguishable from illnesses of a diabolical origin.

Besides a priest exorcist, these people also need a psychologist or a psychiatrist.

How do we proceed in discerning cases that the faithful maintain are the object of the extraordinary action of the Devil?

4

Who Is Attacked

We are all attacked by Satan through his ordinary, devious, and, for this reason, extremely dangerous action: temptation. A life absent of faith—that is, a life lacking or having an incomplete relationship of communion with Jesus—is already fertile ground for an extraordinary action of the Devil. Also, balancing an apparent life of faith with esoteric occult practices and philosophies further leaves a person open to the enemy, allowing him to enter his life and influence it. Other possible initial causes are: participation at séances or even just having assisted at them; associations with wizards, fortune-tellers, or mediums or having personally been involved with their magical or esoteric practices; having made use of amulets and charms, especially if they were obtained from wizards; having brought back from foreign lands objects typical of the local magic; having bought souvenirs or assisted at local magic rituals; having practiced techniques associated with the New Age; having been present at séances in order to receive so-called *healing fluids*; having been part of sects, groups, or associations in which esoteric or occult rites were carried out; having been part of satanic sects or taken part in satanic rites (such as the blood oath drawn up with the demons); having participated in black masses or the voluntary profanation of the Eucharist; having been present at or participated in ritual homicides; having quite frequently listened to very loud music with messages inviting listeners to the cult of Satan or to violence, necrophilia, blasphemy, homicide, suicide, or the so-called alternative religious movements.

A magical and superstitious mentality and adherence to Satan is offensive to God, since on them, the person seeks to find solutions to personal problems through practices, objects, and rituals rather than through absolute faith in Jesus Christ, the only One who can save us and liberate us from suffering and from the Evil One.

It is also important to verify if a person has experienced very traumatic experiences (physical violence, sexual violence, aggressions, accidents, et cetera); if he has grave sins that have never been confessed or insufficiently atoned for (for example, abortion, incest, adultery, sacrilege, homicides, and deviant sexual activity); if he has committed grave injustices and left them unrectified; if he bears hatred or has refused to pardon others, particularly in the family circle or persons close to the family.

It is also useful to investigate the workplace and the social life of the person, since these can reveal relationships or situations that are the cause and origin of difficulties there, such as health problems, a bad attitude, or a poor psychological state of mind, which can tend toward depression and distrust.

Some report feeling persecuted or rejected, feeling unseen and isolated. From the combined practices and experiences of various exorcists, it seems that the possible entrance of the Demon into the life of a person may also be attributed to the spiritual consequences of the person's sins or those of his relatives. It must be clarified, however, that the fault of the sin falls on the one who committed it and not on his descendants or others. A relapse into the sin may occur in the person or the family members if, once it is confessed, there has not been sufficient reparation. All of this indicates a spasmodic and disoriented effort, a kind of do-it-yourself spiritual pursuit that, at times, unconsciously opens the door to the Devil.

Often one confuses spirituality with spiritism. The follower of spiritism believes that with the practice of certain rituals a person can obtain powers that are superior to human nature. These are not expressions of faith. Rather, they are the way one falls into a superstitious mentality and the magical arts.

The latest frontier in this area is the advent of games and apps one can download on cellphones and tablets. In these we find all that is required to put one in contact with spirits that we think are at our service but in reality, in exchange for their powers, take over our human and spiritual life, that is, our body and soul. These apps can make the cell or the tablet a true and proper means (medium) of putting one in contact with the afterlife and with spiritual presences that are actually demons, even in cases in which they do not appear as such, as when they present themselves under the form of angels of God.

But the angels of God cannot contact nor respond to our requests; and if they could, they would be acting in disobedience to God's plan.

In utilizing applications, games, literature, films, and music that invoke or sing praises of spirits and energies, we open the door of our life to malicious forces. These satisfy our curiosity, but their only true goal is that of distancing us from God and of depriving us of physical health in this world and of eternal life in the next. The Devil, the father of lies, the perverse one and the perverter, uses every instrument he can to reach his goal: the destruction of man.

5

How a Person Is Attacked

The actions of the Devil and the experiences of those who are subjected to them are attested by the faith and experience of the Church. Satan and the other rebellious angels are able to interfere in the life of man. To such an end, they can influence thoughts and communicate phrases that the person attacked will not be able to recall. For example: "that one there" (referring to our Lady); "He will not return to you because you are mine"; "Stop praying"; "You cannot do anything"; and when praying, "Now stop it, I am tired"; or provocative discourses, phrases, and insults of a pernicious character that grate on nerves and stir up anger (even more suspicious when coming from a normally mild and respectful person), and so forth.

Other recurring thoughts are "No one understands you"; "No one loves you"; "No one esteems you"; "Only I can help you"; "They are all foolishness" (referring to prayers, the Gospel, and the sacraments); and "You have more important things to do now; you can pray later" (as a result, one does not pray). There are also thoughts of suicide, solitude, bewilderment, loss of meaning, hatred toward dear ones, deep discomfort, interior malaise, and so forth.

Satan can also use sensibilities, fear and interior fragility, or psychic disturbances as doors through which to arrive at the will and spirit of the person he attacks.

The enemy can so influence a person's reactions, phrases, and thoughts that he then does not recall saying or doing them. It can happen that the phrases of the Evil One alternate with those of the person being confused, and he does not understand the reason it is happening. The person can become extremely talkative (logorrheic), to the extent that it provokes nervousness and hatred. By utilizing a person's hidden weaknesses, anxieties, and fears, the Evil One amplifies them and makes them recurring and obsessive. For example, when one prays, he is assaulted by a deep sleepiness, yawns that dislocate the jaw, and persistent coughs. A person can become convinced that dreams experienced between sleep and waking were real events; or he may experience sudden nightly awakenings that, at times, recur at precise hours. The Demon attacks in a deceitful way those who have made use of the occult and esoteric arts, generating premonitory dreams or visions during the night or day, passing on knowledge of the occult, and empowering the hands to cure illnesses and the mind to predict the future. At the same time, he can instill in such persons the belief that these "gifts" are given to do good.

The actions of the powers of darkness on man's interior life can occur on two levels: through temptation, which is the ordinary action (Jesus let Himself be tempted) and through the extraordinary action, the stronger, more direct action.

The ordinary action of the Devil: temptation

Temptation is an action through which a person is put to the test (with good or with bad intentions). Diabolical temptation is the Devil's way of seeking man's eternal ruin. In it, we recognize a number of phases.

  1. *Suggestion* excites the imagination, the memory (in recalling past situations and actions), the senses, the

passions, the aspirations, and even projects. Here de-monic action can be powerful.

2. *Delight* proceeds from the pleasure presented by the suggestion.

3. *Consent* alone renders the situation sinful. Even if man does not lose his liberty, his will can be weakened or influenced by suggestion and delight.

By the will of God, man cannot be tempted beyond his strength; therefore, he is able to conquer temptation if he does not lose his constant reference to Jesus and thus obedience to God. The enemy works his temptations at the level of the will and free will with the weapons of seduction, fear, confusion, disorder, and lies. He tries to sow doubt about God's love and His desire to help man fulfill his life and liberty. Doubt works to turn temptation into disobedience and then sin. Through disobedience and sin, Satan can enter into the will and the free will of the one he has snared and bring him ever deeper into the darkness of error and eternal death.

The extraordinary action of the Devil

Satan's other action in this world is extraordinary action, which God permits in some cases for reasons known only to Him. The Gospel speaks clearly of the character of a diabolical presence in man, who becomes like a "house" that has been usurped by an enemy and taken over. (Mark 3:22–27 mentions exorcisms worked by Jesus.) Extraordinary diabolical action is manifested in various forms that bear the names of vexation, obsession, possession, and infestation.

Diabolical vexation

Diabolical vexations that appear as physical attacks on a person are cuts, burns, scratches, punctures, writing on the skin, bites, beatings, blows that leave bruises, swellings, bloody sores, broken bones, incisions on the skin that spell words or form signs that persist for a certain time and then disappear, and illnesses with unknown causes and unknown cures. Obstacles also occur in the workplace and among affective relationships without logical explanation.

In the lives of the saints, other, even more serious, forms of vexations have been noted. Some of the saints have been the targets of stones, excrement, and feces that seemed to have come out of nowhere. Others have been hurled from their beds or down the stairs, tossed in the air or thrown down to the floor or against a wall, or dragged by the hair by an invisible hand; others have been taken from where they were and transported long distances.

In some cases, especially when the demon attacks physically, discernment is extremely easy. In these forms of vexation, the person attacked does not always manifest a repugnance toward the sacred or toward God. We have seen an example of this in the life of St. Pio of Pietrelcina and in so many other saints who have been subjected to physical vexations.

Evaluation by the priest exorcist is particularly challenging. He must listen to and evaluate persons tormented by certain symptoms or who are worn down by a chain reaction of negative events, such as misfortunes, failures, or physical illnesses, and are convinced that they need the exorcist priest. In these cases, the exorcist can assume that there is extraordinary demonic action if he can ascertain a connection between the possible effects previously described and an unexplainable aversion toward God, prayer, and the sacred.

If, together with the intensification of blessings and prayers of liberation, one sees a significant reduction of such phenomena, then one can suspect that their origin is in the extraordinary action of the devil.

Diabolical obsession

There are demonic assaults that, although they do not block the person's intellectual powers and free will, succeed in inserting thoughts or obsessive images into the mind (the imagination and the memory) that the victim is not able to expel. In these cases, the person feels tormented by a fixed idea that he knows is foreign to him and seeks to find a way to reject it. But it is so deeply imprinted in his mind and spirit that it seems to be really his.

Obsessions can take on diverse forms, levels, and intensities and finally completely dominate the mind of the person. In that case, they become very strong and prolonged. To avoid confusing them with psychiatric pathologies, some exorcists prefer to define them with the term *mental or psychic demonic vexations* or *interior demonic vexations*; others prefer the term *personal demonic infestations*. Nevertheless, it is possible that the action of the Devil and a real psychic illness are present contemporaneously.

Given their similarity to psychiatric illnesses, the detection of diabolical obsessions is not always easy. The majority of these cases are pathological. There are some, however, that although manifesting themselves as symptoms similar to a psychiatric pathology, have their origin in an extraordinary action of the Devil.

Finally, others, although pathological, are amplified abnormally by an extraordinary action of the demon. In this last case, little obsessive thoughts and modest compulsive behaviors (normal when they are healthy and controllable)[27] suddenly become

---

[27] There are those who continually check to see if the lights or the gas burners are turned off. Some have an exaggerated mania for clean hands or are continually washing up. Here the Devil is not concerned. Then there are distracted individuals who do

invasive, troubling, and continuous. Therefore, an unbalanced or hysterical subject can be a victim of a diabolical obsession, which ends with superimposing itself on the psychiatric illness, worsening his condition. For all these reasons, the field of demonic obsessions is one of the most difficult to evaluate.

Physical diabolical vexations and possessions usually are easily identifiable by their external signs. To arrive at concrete conclusions, each case must be examined individually. As previously mentioned, a significant sign of the origin of an obsession is the presence of a block, partial or total, toward prayer, or an unmotivated hatred toward everything that is sacred or has a reference toward the sacred.

But it is not always like this. At times persons who pray and regularly receive the sacraments (and do not present the above-mentioned symptoms and attitudes) can be subjected to obsessive forms of evil origins.

We see it in the lives of the saints when they are obsessed by the thought or sensation of being damned. Therefore, it is necessary to realize that there are situations in which it is possible to make a discernment of an obsession of the extraordinary action of the Devil by observing the efficacy or nonefficacy of the blessings and prayers of liberation. If the obsessions persist, it is better to send the person to an exorcist. When an extraordinary diabolical action is superimposed on a pathological obsession,

---

a task mechanically and then ask if they turned off the lights, washed their hands before eating, et cetera. They have to go back over their steps. These things happen because they are overly anxious or their memory is weak, but it is not a demonic obsession. These things are conquered in part with good sense, in part with accepting them.

it is necessary to intervene with both medical therapy and an exorcism.

Diabolical possession

Possession is not a splitting of the personality, as occurs in the case of a mental illness. Rather, it involves a temporary displacement of the person, during which a brutal and violent demonic spirit takes control. Acting from within the body, the demon makes the helpless victim speak and act as he wishes: such a phenomenon can be defined as the *moment of crisis*.

The Devil dominates the body of the person in order to annul his faculties of self-determination and control. The presence of the demon in the human body neutralizes the person's ability to direct himself, so that he becomes a blind, docile instrument that is fatally obedient to a perverse and despotic power.

Thus, there are two components to the diabolical possession of a human body: the presence of the demon in the body and the exercise of his power. As such, the person possessed could be moved to another place, raised up, or temporarily changed physically.

During the crises, the person can be conscious, semiconscious, or in a total trance. In the exorcistic rite of 1952, the phenomena that accompany the possession are described as the speaking of a language completely unknown, possessing superhuman strength, bodily levitation, a change in physical features or characteristics, alteration of the voice, furious reactions before sacred objects, convulsions, loud cries, blasphemies, and the knowledge of things regarding the occult. Periods of calm can alternate with periods of crisis. The latter generally occur before sacred objects.

Prudence is necessary in determining the actuality of a possession. The possessed person is not responsible for acts committed while he is under diabolical influences. Possession is Satan's supreme act of power, which he employs to demonstrate his superiority over man and his rebellion against God.

Regarding cases of persons who simultaneously manifest psychiatric disturbances and extraordinary phenomena, human deliberation does not have sufficient resources to justify a priori the exclusion of a probable demonic possession. Therefore, it is necessary to conduct a careful interdisciplinary examination that includes specialists in both the medical and spiritual fields. In this situation, the exorcist—assisted by medical specialists—determines the real causes and various components of the person's illness.

In the Gospel, some cases of possession are clearly described: the mute demoniac (Matt. 9:32–33); the blind, mute demoniac who gives origin to the controversy with the Pharisees (Matt. 12:22–32; Mark 3:20–30; Luke 11:14–26); and Mary Magdalene (Mark 16:9; Luke 8:2). Four cases are described in detail: the demoniac of Capernaum (Mark 1:21–28; Luke 4:31–37); the demoniacs of Gerasa (Matt. 8:28–34; Mark 5:1–20; Luke 8:26–29); the daughter of the Canaanite woman (Matt. 15:21–28; Mark 7:24–30); and the epileptic child (Matt. 17:14–20; Mark 9:14–28; Luke 9:37–43).

In these situations, Jesus reveals the motive for His presence in the history of men: to bring about the salvation and the liberation of man from the forces of the Evil One. He makes the Apostles and all the believers in Him who work in His name (Mark 16:17) collaborators in His work of salvation, conferring on them the power of crushing demons (Matt. 10:1–8; Mark 3:14–15; 6:7; Luke 9:1; 10:17–20).

In the Acts of the Apostles we find testimonies of the expulsion of the demons in virtue of such a mandate (5:14–16; 8:5–8; 16:16–18; 19:11–16).

In tormenting humans whom he hates, the Devil can feel solely a very wretched type of satisfaction because it does not diminish his torments, nor does God permit him to destroy man.

One cannot speak of a predisposition to possession, physical, psychic, or moral. Obstinate sinners are already victims of the Devil and they have no need of particular influences, whereas, once possessed, they would not voluntarily offend the Lord.

Vexation and possession are not per se a moral evil; rather, they are physical evils that God also permits for the good of the person. Some theologians point out the reasons for that divine permission: (1) for an increase in God's glory (in this way God manifests His love and His attributes); (2) in order to manifest a truth of the Catholic religion, which is endowed with a special divine power; (3) for the spiritual profit of the upright; (4) as beneficial teachings for man; and (5) as proof for the conversion of sinners.

Diabolical infestation of a locality

The extraordinary action of the Devil that causes disturbances and nuisances in places, houses, and objects is called diabolical infestation in a locality. It also includes diabolical action on animals, which, in the last analysis is directed at man. The manifestations of such action are unexplainable noises, apparitions of objects or changes of their location, music or odd noises, phosphorescence (emission of light without any perceptible heat), odors, lights, animals that react as if they have seen someone or that are in an excited state, shadows, silhouettes, faces, and so forth.

Disturbances caused by these demonic interventions are carried out with noises or blows on the roof, pavement, walls, doors, windows, or furniture; showers of hailstones that fall as from nowhere on the roof or even in the house; noises of invisible steps, fireworks, or explosives; the clanging of chains and irons; mysterious voices, cries, laughs, or uproars; invisible bells that clamor; the disappearance of objects that are never found again or are found in the most unusual places in the house; pictures that are detached from the walls and fall without a comprehensible reason; underwear, sheets, blankets, and chairs that levitate in the air; animals (such as ravens, bats, reptiles, owls, dogs, or cats) that suddenly appear and soon vanish; sudden, intense, and untraceable burnt odors of excrement, sulfur, rotting flesh, or incense; and so forth.

If, after a vigorous inquiry, natural causes are excluded, prayers, blessings, and celebrations of Masses (authorized by the bishop) are offered in that place. If that leads to a disappearance of the phenomena or a significant lessening of them, one can suspect that their origin was truly an extraordinary action of the demon. At times infestations of such phenomena disappear, not because of blessings and exorcisms, but rather because their demonic origin is in someone who lives in that place and the phenomena are tied to that person. Once that person changes habitation, those who continue to live there no longer notice anything and live peacefully. The unexplainable phenomena follow the afflicted party to his new domicile.

6

Signs of the Extraordinary
Action of Satan

Signs of the extraordinary action of Satan can take place in a
person, in a place, or in a home. These signs have precise characteristics. They do not have a rational or causal explanation.
Moreover, they usually are cyclical in their repetition in time
and in their recurrence on specific dates or important events in
the life of the person attacked.

Such signs of the extraordinary action of Satan need to be
verified through the prayers of the Church and the victim, who
must follow a life of communion with God and be reconciled
in the sacrament of Penance and reinforced with the Eucharist,
the Bread of Life.

Regarding the person attacked, signs that can arouse suspicions are difficulty in praying owing to strong yawns, headache,
cold chills, distraction, profound discomfort, and nausea; im-
pulses to vomit; refusal of sacred objects and objects of devotion; invasive and recurring thoughts of desperation, distrust,
finding pain in living; having visions; doubting the love of God;
experiencing imaginings; tremors or sudden illnesses that have
no effective cure; states of sudden and unexpected anger; feelings of profound and violent hate; fear or depression without
immediate or comprehensible cause; visual hallucinations with

perceptions of nonexistent objects; hallucinations of various sounds, noises, and voices; olfactory hallucinations with the perception of often unpleasant odors such as rotten eggs or sulfur; illusions; deformed perceptions of something that exists; delirium; premonitions of things that will happen; warning dreams, knowledge of hidden things and the occult; sudden voice changes; modification of facial features; unexplainable obstacles at work; and family divisions that are perpetuated from generation to generation.

We must specify that some of these symptoms and phenomena are also common to psychic disturbances—psychological and psychiatric—which have nothing to do with the extraordinary action of the Evil One. In some cases, as has been confirmed by some exorcists, they are concomitant with the extraordinary action of Satan or they are a problem in which the Evil One takes cover and finds strength. Once the human psyche has been healed, the extraordinary diabolical action emerges, and with prayer the spiritual disturbances will also be resolved.

In these cases, collaboration between the priest exorcist and the medical specialist is extremely necessary.

Places and habitations are the second ambit for the extraordinary action of the Evil One. It must be stated in advance that at times the phenomena that occur there are tied to the presence of cursed objects, which guarantee the presence of the powers of darkness. Until such objects are removed from the house, the phenomena will remain (even if the exorcist's prayer attenuates the effects). At other times, the phenomena are caused by the presence in the house of a person with spiritual disturbances. The proof lies in the fact that wherever the person goes, the phenomena and signs of the extraordinary action of the demon remain with him. These phenomena are expressions of the power that the Evil One uses to depress, discourage, intimidate, and disorient the person he attacks.

Signs of the extraordinary action of the demon in a place, as previously mentioned, are blows on walls and in wardrobes and closets, the sound of footsteps, the shuffling of furniture, the dragging of chains, the opening of doors and drawers, the turning on and off of gas burners, the opening and closing of shutters, the plummeting of the temperature of the house in spite of a functional heating system, bad odors, the movement of objects, and their disappearance or discovery in unusual places. When these phenomena are perceived by several occupants of the house, it is evident that they are not the fruit of imagination or hallucinations.

There are cases in which objects that do not belong to the person or to the other inhabitants of the house—objects such as braids, plumes, garlands, ropes, hairs, or threads of various colors—are found in pillows or mattresses. Other objects may appear on the floors of closets, among clothing in drawers, on the floor, or on the furniture. Stains or holes may also appear inexplicably on clothing, curtains, blankets, or sheets.

In general, the demon uses all these phenomena to persuade us that God has abandoned us or that we are powerless before the forces of evil. Satan tries to make us doubt that we are loved and protected by God. These extraordinary actions generate various reactions in the persons attacked, including fear, anxiety, bewilderment, disorder, difficulty praying or in approaching the sacraments, desperation, and even thoughts of suicide.

God does not ever abandon us, not even when we are in the state of sin.

To the contrary, we are the ones who easily abandon God and accuse Him of leaving us alone in our difficulties. Jesus affirms:

"Lo, I am with you always, to the close of the age" (Matt. 28:20); "In the world you have tribulation; but be of good cheer, I have overcome the world" (John 16:33); "I saw Satan fall like lightning from heaven. Behold, I have given you authority to tread upon serpents and scorpions, and over all the power of the enemy; and nothing shall hurt you. Nevertheless do not rejoice in this, that the spirits are subject to you; but rejoice that your names are written in heaven" (Luke 10:19–20). We must not fear Satan but neither should we underestimate him. We have seen that the Evil One is man's only and most powerful enemy. He is able to bring us to perdition and distance our soul from God. But through the Holy Spirit, Jesus has given us the weapons to combat the Evil One.

Part 3

Weapons to Use
Against the Devil

The arms of combat against the forces of evil must be used by Christians in their totality and unity. Above all, a *habitus* is necessary; that is, a way of thinking, loving, and acting that conforms to the life of Jesus. A simple and humble soul totally confident in God—as Jesus had in his earthly life—learns how to relate to our Creator. The freedom to choose enables man to resist the Devil, because the Devil can tempt us, but he can never oblige us to do his will.

The arms of combat and defense that Jesus has left us consist of the Word of God, prayer, fasting, and the sacraments.

In using these weapons of defense, we must guard against a superstitious attitude toward their efficacy; that would be a magical concept. In other words, we must not believe that our religious practices dispel demons. On the basis of biblical testimony, the Devil is expelled solely by faith and total trust in Jesus. Our Lady and all the saints show us how communion with God makes the human being, a creature inferior to Satan, stronger than the Satan himself. This accelerates the Evil One's intense hostility toward man, which he puts in motion when the person he has attacked decides to return to God with all his being through the use of these weapons.

7

The Word of God, the Gospel

The Word of God listened to consistently and repeatedly in the course of the day is the inspiration and the weapon that over-comes doubts, anxieties, recurring thoughts, fits of depression, suicide, anger, confusion, and all the disorder that Satan can generate in the mind. Indeed, the attack of the Evil One begins by penetrating the core of the will and the free will—the mind and the intelligence—influencing and subjugating them until he can arrive at the soul and then accompany it to evil.

Often those who go to a priest exorcist are prayerful, go to Mass on Sunday and sometimes also during the week, but they complain of sudden awakenings at night, tormenting dreams and obsessive recurring thoughts, doubts about God and their faith in Him. It must be emphasized that these persons do not participate or assist at esoteric rituals, not even as a joke. Usually, however, they are lacking in involvement with the Word of God, that is, with Jesus Christ, the center and foundation of the Christian life, Jesus Christ, the Word of God.

In the Gospel of Luke, after Jesus was baptized and led by the Spirit of God into the desert, He was tempted by Satan. In that case, victory over the demon did not occur through prayer. Three times Jesus cited Sacred Scripture in order to resist the temptations and refute the lies of the enemy. Jesus affirmed: "It is written ..." (Luke 4:1–13). The Word of God

9

was His instrument of truth against the lies and provocations of the enemy.

Jesus, in making Himself man, became one like us to show us how to keep the enemy away. He kept His distance from Satan, citing the source of wisdom and discernment: the Word of God. And He teaches us that, in order to bear our earthly life with serenity, it is always necessary to have His words in mind, so that in every adversity the Word of God comes to our mind and, guided by the Holy Spirit, we may know how to choose what is true and good. It is fundamental that the Gospel be imprinted on our mind, the seat of the will and of free will. Satan knows that if he succeeds in confusing the free will by turning it aside and distancing it from the will of God through sin, he can also corrupt and damage the soul of man. The Word of God listened to and lived each day in concrete choices becomes our defense from the snares of the Evil One.

8

Prayer

We often take for granted that we know what prayer is, but in reality we do not. From childhood, we were taught to say prayers in the morning and in the evening, but perhaps we did not understand the value or the meaning of it.

At the Last Supper Jesus said: "This cup which is poured out for you is the new covenant in my blood" (Luke 22:20). With these words, Jesus is telling us that God the Father has established an eternal alliance with man, a relationship of faith founded on the sacrifice of Christ on the Cross. This alliance is maintained only if, through the Gospel, there is a response from man. This response occurs in prayer that has been stirred up by the teaching of the Word of God. To pray is to converse with God after having listened to Him. Jesus tells us: "You did not choose me, but I chose you" (John 15:16).

Prayer is also praise and thanksgiving. This is the prayer Jesus prefers: that He is thanked continuously for life, for what we are, and for what we have.

Prayer is also an invocation or supplication for help. If it bursts from a soul purified by the sacrament of Reconciliation, the prayer is immediately heard because the person praying is in communion with Jesus and He is particularly attentive to humble souls (Luke 18:7–8). The Word is not only a voice; it is a person in flesh and blood, God Himself made man in the person of Jesus (John

12:44–45, 48–50). To listen to Jesus is to listen to the Invisible One, the Omnipotent One, the One made visible and reachable.

Prayer manifests trust, confidence, supplication, praise, and joy and is expressed not only in words but, above all, in the disposition of the soul. Prayer is more effective when it has a precise intention and demonstrates communion with God. In this way, it becomes a force against instinctive states such as solitude, fear, anxiety, confusion, and disorder; and it places everything under the guidance of Jesus, who helps us to overcome human weaknesses and the temptations of the Evil One.

Our prayer, however, cannot be a direct instrument of liberation from the enemy, since we cannot combat him by ourselves. As human creatures, we are weaker beings, inferior to the angelic creatures. To believe that we can liberate ourselves from the Evil One solely through our own prayer would be a sin of arrogance, since we cannot expel the Evil One with our own strength alone. Indeed, by driving away the enemy, we would be making his wickedness even more effective in our life. Therefore, it is only prayer that can expel the demon—that is, insofar as it is a call for the intervention of Jesus, Mary, and the saints.

At times, we might offer a prayer of benediction or liberation and it is not heard. It is not because of our spiritual condition at that particular moment that our prayer seems ineffectual; in reality, it is our unpardoned sin that impedes the action of God.

I have been able to verify through the persons I assist that the majority of spiritual disturbances occur through the conduct of a muddled or hypocritical spiritual life, that is, through inconstancy in prayer, inconstancy in the encounter with Jesus in the sacraments, and inconstancy in listening to the Word of God. In these cases, to assist our prayer, it is helpful to become familiar with a suitable catechism and to receive the sacrament of Reconciliation. The efficacy of this last remedy depends on a coherent and faithful Christian life.

If prayer springs forth from a soul in communion with God, it is immediately effective against the attacks of the enemy. I had the case of a man who suddenly went from extremely devout to refusing the sacred. His sister, also very faithful, pointed out this apparently unexplainable change. I counseled her to invoke mentally the intervention of Mary Immaculate precisely at the moment of her brother's visceral anger. She told me that, as a result of the prayer, her brother calmed down at times and at times grew worse. This was proof that the change was not chosen by the brother; rather, it was the consequence of the Devil's vexation. The brother, in fact, was not able to know about his sister's mental prayer.

There was also the case of a five-year-old boy whose mother had taught him how to pray the Hail Mary. I was called because the child saw shadows around his bed. I told the parents to maintain themselves in the state of grace with God through the sacrament of Reconciliation in order to render the prayer more powerful, and that, when this phenomenon reoccurred, to invoke the intervention of our Mother in Heaven. After a week they called me, saying that the phenomenon was reduced but not ended. I asked if they had prayed with the boy. They said no. I invited them to pray with him when the phenomenon occurred. They did. They told me that as soon as the child said "Hail," the shadows no longer returned. That "Hail" alone prayed by the little child in trust and in genuine and total faith was enough to chase away the powers of darkness.

The *Catechism of the Catholic Church* reminds us that

to attribute the efficacy of prayers or of sacramental signs to their mere external performance, apart from the interior dispositions they demand, is to fall into superstition (cf. Matt. 23:16–22). (no. 2111)

The prayer that comes forth from a humble heart and is in communion with God is not only efficacious; it also becomes an instrument of perception for unmasking the enemy and his actions.

9

The Sacraments

In Latin, the word *sacrament* is composed of two parts: *sacrum* and *signum* (sacred sign). Unlike a sacramental (prayer, blessing) that *expresses faith*, a sacrament is the sacred sign of the *presence and action of God*. A sacrament works in the fullness of grace, obtaining for us communion with God in the truth and strength of the Holy Spirit, who is present in us from our Baptism. The sacraments are a relationship with God founded on the encounter with Jesus. They guide the spiritual life.

A relationship with God is based on three activities: listening, through the Gospel; dialogue, through prayer; and the encounter with Jesus, through the sacraments. If we are deprived of even one of these three, our connection with God is undermined and weakened. The sacraments of Reconciliation and the Eucharist maintain our identity and dignity as children of God. It is beneficial to use them often. The sacrament of Reconciliation well lived (with humble recognition and repentance of sins before Jesus) is more efficacious than an exorcism, which is only a sacramental. In the sacrament of Reconciliation, God receives us as Father. Humbling ourselves before God distances us from the arrogance, pride, and egoism taught to us by Satan.

In the Eucharist, we encounter Jesus the sacrament, the *Bread of Life* for the soul. Without the Eucharist, the soul is weakened because it does not have the spiritual strength that flows from the sacrament. The Eucharist is the sign of God's mercy toward man because it is the fruit of the Passion and death of Jesus, the sacrifice of salvation. To receive the Eucharist is to receive Jesus in one's life. In the Eucharist, He invites us to offer to God, out of love for Him and for our neighbor, the breaking of the bread and the pouring of the wine.

In many cases, one notices a total liberation from the snares of the enemy solely by putting one's spiritual life in order; that is, through living the Faith in the grace of God and with the regular reception of the sacraments.

10

Faith and the Spiritual Life

Exorcism and sacramentals in general (prayers, blessings with water, oil, blessed salt, blessed objects, and relics) have their value, but if we think that only these may obtain liberation, we fall into grave error. Those who suffer from extraordinary diabolical phenomena must be aware that liberation depends principally on conversion of the heart and living a life of total faith in Jesus Christ. If the serious sins of one's life are not eliminated through Confession, even participation at Holy Mass can become a sacrament of condemnation. Citing Sacred Scripture, the *Catechism* affirms in this regard:

> The Lord addresses an invitation to us, urging us to receive him in the sacrament of the Eucharist: "Truly, I say to you, unless you eat the flesh of the Son of man and drink his blood, you have no life in you" (John 6:53). To respond to this invitation we must *prepare ourselves* for so great and so holy a moment. St. Paul urges us to examine our conscience: "Whoever, therefore, eats the bread or drinks the cup of the Lord in an unworthy manner will be guilty of profaning the body and blood of the Lord. Let a man examine himself, and so eat of the bread and drink of the cup. For any one who eats and drinks without discerning the body eats and drinks judgment upon

himself" (1 Cor. 11:27–29). Anyone conscious of a grave sin must receive the sacrament of Reconciliation before coming to communion.

Before so great a sacrament, the faithful can only echo humbly and with ardent faith the words of the Centurion: *"Domine, non sum dignus ut intres sub tectum meum, sed tantum dic verbo, et sanabitur anima mea"* ("Lord, I am not worthy that you should enter under my roof, but only say the word and my soul will be healed"). (nos. 1384–1386)[28]

If prayers of liberation and exorcism procure only slight spiritual improvements in a person, it is necessary to ask oneself if there is a real conversion of heart or a religious pedantry.

Through divine permission, some of the faithful (including laymen and consecrated religious) are called by God to cooperate

---

[28] *Roman Missal*, response to the invitation to Communion; cf. Matt. 8:8. In the *Summa Theologica*, St. Thomas Aquinas says: "One sin can be said to be graver than another in two ways: first of all essentially, secondly accidentally. Essentially, in regard to its species, which is taken from its object: and so a sin is greater according as that against which it is committed is greater. And since Christ's Godhead is greater than His humanity, and His humanity greater than the sacraments of His humanity, hence it is that those are the gravest sins which are committed against the Godhead, such as unbelief and blasphemy. The second degree of gravity is held by those sins which are committed against His humanity: hence it is written (Matt. 12:32): And anyone who says a word against the Son of Man will be forgiven; but no one who speaks against the Holy Spirit will be forgiven either in this world or in the next." In the third part, finally, are the sins committed against the sacraments, which are linked to the humanity of Christ, and after these the sins against simple creatures" (III, Q. 80, art. 5).

in the salvation of humanity through sufferings that are derived from vexations, obsessions, or, at times, even demonic possessions. Satan does not fear exorcisms as much as he fears the humble and pure disposition with which these faithful receive the rite of exorcism. Therefore, each one who is struck must cultivate a heartfelt trust in the mercy of God and must exercise mercy toward his neighbor, pardoning unconditionally and loving his enemies. He must also take care to guard his tongue, to avoid grumbling, gossiping, and making contemptuous assertions about his neighbors, above all about the ones who have offended him. He must be aware, as St. Faustina Kowalska is in her diary, that, "The tongue is a small organ, but it does big things.... There is life but there is also death in the tongue. Sometimes we kill with the tongue; we commit real murders."[29] The person being exorcised must avoid gossip and exercise self-control in the presence of persons who criticize, to avoid being dragged into vicious circles of judgments. When he is experiencing the greatest torments from the assaults of the Evil One, he must ask God for peace of heart and offer Him his own suffering with complete trust. The person being exorcised will know with certainty that God will give him all that is necessary to resist temptation.

On the path to liberation, prayer is equally important, although secondary to the will that must always conform to the will of God. Unfortunately, some persons seen by exorcists do not pray; they limit themselves to some salutary daily invocations, even though their condition requires a life of intense prayer and a deep love for the will of God. They do not pray out of a lack of time or because they have not understood the purifying and transforming effects of prayer; rather, in certain cases they are

---

[29] *Divine Mercy in my Soul*, p. 118.

impeded by the demon. Regarding the necessity of prayer, St. Faustina Kowalska affirms:

> A soul arms itself by prayer for all kinds of combat. In whatever state the soul might be, it ought to pray. A soul which is pure and beautiful must pray, or else it will lose its beauty; a soul which is striving after such purity must pray, or else it will never attain it; a soul which is newly converted must pray, or else it will fall again; a soul plunged in sins must pray, so that it might rise again. There is no soul which is not bound to pray, for every grace comes to the soul through prayer.... Let the soul be aware that in order to pray and persevere in prayer, it must arm itself with patience and cope bravely with exterior and interior difficulties. Interior difficulties are discouragement, spiritual dryness, heaviness of spirit, and temptations; exterior difficulties are human respect and time set apart for prayer. This has been my personal experience because, when I did not pray at the time assigned for prayer, later on I could not do it because of my duties; or if I did manage to do so, it was only with great difficulty, because my thoughts kept wandering off to my duties.[30]

Let us also remember that, in the spiritual life of a Christian, and especially in those who experience extraordinary attacks by the Devil, one cannot neglect the frequent use of the sacraments. Divine mercy is present thanks to the sacraments. We exorcists can verify that the sacrament of Confession is particularly feared and hated by the demon, because it snatches from him so many souls.

[30] Ibid., pp. 146–147.

When man humbly and sincerely recognizes his sins, repents, and confesses them, he does what the demon in his inordinate pride will never do: he humiliates himself before God; he recognizes that God is the Creator and Lord and that he is a creature of God, ever in need of His mercy. This behavior permits us to be received into the merciful arms of Christ, who immerses us in His blood and purifies us from all the stains of sin. Thus, having been renewed, each Christian (and even more so, the person being exorcised), nourished and reinforced by receiving Jesus in the Eucharist, engages with new vigor in his battle against the Evil One.

Participation at Holy Mass becomes a great work of mercy for us if it is lived as an offering for neighbors, living or dead. St. Veronica Giuliani provides us with an example of this love offering. She makes us understand how seeking intimate union with Jesus' love for us enables us to conquer the temptations of the Evil One.

St. Veronica is relevant because she listened to Love speaking to her heart—to Jesus—and it bore fruit, thrilling and animating her soul. The entire life of St. Veronica was lived as a witness to the truth of God's Word. In her diary she writes principally of the beauty of being loved by Jesus:

> It seemed to me that our Lord was at the door of my heart, telling me repeatedly, "Open for me, open for me." These calls made me exult with joy and I, addressing my Lord, told him that for him my door was never closed, asking him to come in because I could no longer wait! He made me understand that he wished to enter but on condition that he be alone and that that domain belong solely to Him. Listening to these invitations and seeing how the

Lord's love takes possession of a soul, I felt my heart palpitating with such vehemence and joy that it seemed to yearn to burst open so that the Lord could make his entry forever.

St. Veronica's last words summarize an existence entirely centered on the desire and search for union with God, her spouse: "Tell everyone! This is the secret of my joy and my sufferings: Love has made itself known to me."

The awareness of being loved by Jesus determines the quality of life of the believer as a child of God and enables him to distance himself from the Evil One and expel him from his life.

In addressing the necessary spiritual formation of the exorcist and the person being exorcised, it is necessary to emphasize that the exorcist must not occupy himself principally with administering exorcisms, but rather in curing his own spiritual life and that of the afflicted person. He must also teach the person to become the exorcist of himself. This does not mean that the exorcistate must assist the exorcist; rather, he himself must oppose the demon with all the means mentioned above. When the person being exorcised has the correct spiritual disposition, the exorcisms will produce a progressive sanctification as well as a gradual liberation.

11

The Ecclesial Community: The Parish

To conquer solitude, self-isolation, diffidence toward others, and distrust toward oneself and toward others, which, at times, is caused by the evil action, it is necessary to be inserted into a community and to feel a sense of belonging to it.

When we are born, we are not alone: we are inserted into a social context, a web of interpersonal relationships, situations, and material things. This also happens at our Baptism: we are welcomed into the community of the family of God, composed of baptized persons. We are the Church gathered together and guided by the Holy Spirit, who works everything in everyone (1 Cor. 12:5).

The Church, because she is composed of sinners, is on a journey toward sanctity and therefore perfectible. Yet, it is into this community that Jesus chose to call to Himself the twelve apostles, simple fishermen. Therefore, we must not be scandalized if, at the core of our parishes, we find careerists (the sons of Zebedee: Matt. 20:20–21); traitors (Judas was a traitor: John 13:21–27); the unreliable and cowardly (Peter and all the disciples: Luke 22:57–58); and backbiters and criticizers (the disciples themselves: Luke 9:49–50).

There is only one Master we must listen to and follow: Jesus Christ. By His side, we must struggle anywhere the Kingdom of God is established. Our struggle is against the Evil One, the one who is trying to destroy communion and peace. Thus, the parish becomes an arena—the meeting place where the Spirit of God exercises His action on me. There the way of the Cross teaches me humility and simplicity and, as a result, conquers my pride and diabolical doubts. Through the parish community I have the possibility of strengthening my soul with the grace of God received in the sacraments.

Remaining in the ecclesial community is also beneficial to our human and relational elements. We do not fall into temptations of voluntary isolationism and diffidence toward our neighbor that in their most serious forms become pathological, making us feel persecuted and attacked. The enemy, in fact, in order to weaken his victim and take possession of him so that he may lead him to an eternal death, seeks to divide him from affections by causing him to doubt friendships and God's love for each man.

12

An Original Instrument of Spiritual Defense

Good music can also be an instrument of spiritual defense. Today's music is diverse in its classification and execution. Within this diversity, there are subjective criteria that influence our choice of music.

Music is pleasing and helpful to a person when its selection is the fruit of objective discernment. When it is chosen merely according to a person's tastes or attitudes, it risks being unwholesome. Studies have proven that music can be an instrument of relaxation and concentration, but it can also be a source of indoctrination, influencing a person's mood and choices through subliminal messages contained in the lyrics or in frequencies that can affect the psyche.

Music can be an instrument that promotes unity, but also incitement of the masses. It is enough to think of national anthems or military marches. In this context, we can include the *rave* (part of the acid movement of the late 1980s), lyric opera performances, symphonic concerts, musical films, and sound tracks.

Which of us, at least once, has not felt emotions listening to music? This is proof of how music can penetrate our soul. The Evil One also makes use of this channel to influence the free will and the mind, in order by means of them to reach the soul.

Particular categories of music that appear innocuous can be doors through which Satan enters into the thoughts, habits, behaviors, and life of the one who listens to them: hard rock, metal, acid rock, and similar genres. Common characteristics of these types of music are fixed and repetitive sounds, high volume, and frenetic rhythms and screams. In some cases, hymns praising Satan are surreptitiously inserted into the verse, making it possible to have more than one interpretation. Such forms of music can involve satanic forms that sweeten the entrance of the Evil One. Among them is the music of the New Age, with sounds of nature played on string or wind instruments, and Eastern music, with string instruments that accompany repetition. In reality, some are evocations of spirits.

A *dialogue* is created between a musical performance and its listeners. Music with its content can create a virtual world in which one finds refuge or identity.

Good music contributes to the growth of the personality when it respects and values human life and when it is free from every form of alienation or exaltation. Good music puts us in contact with one another when it is rooted in objective, absolute, universal, and infallible values, characteristics that reside solely in God.

It is necessary, then, to be attentive to the content of the words and the frequencies and rhythms of music to distinguish the aggressive, the violent, the illusory, and the deceitful from what is relaxing and edifying. In some cases, constant listening to certain kinds of music can generate aggressive attitudes and a state of mind or logic that is violent and repressive.

For good music, we suggest a selection of songs with lyrics from Sacred Scripture or hymns in praise of God. A prayer set to music is particularly helpful to a person who is withdrawn, depressed, or having difficulty with prayer. Some vexed or possessed persons who have been made to listen to good music have received profound benefits in their souls and serenity in their lives. Music's effect cannot be undervalued, whether in one's behavior or in one's way of thinking and loving; but above all, in the way it reaches the human soul.

Part 4

Discerning and Accompanying

In this chapter we shall try to understand the kind of spiritual help a pastor or relative can offer to persons who say they have spiritual problems.

Such persons can be lost, confused, and spiritually or physically ill. They need charity and multiple cures, physical or mental, or both. Those who have spiritual problems need serenity of spirit, and patience in facing them.

The one who helps and the one who is helped must never forget that Jesus Christ has conquered Satan and has definitively broken the power of the spirit of the Evil One (see Col. 2:15; Eph. 1:21; Rev. 12:7–12). Jesus is "the stronger man" who conquered the "strong man" (see Luke 11:22). With the power of the Spirit, the Holy One and Sanctifier, he ceaselessly continues this victorious work. In Him, the Conqueror, we also have won. For the one who is rooted in Christ, there is no reason for a paralyzing fear of the Devil. The struggle against evil continuously engages the believer, but now there is no longer reason for desperation; evil has already been defeated, its power limited, and its end established.

13

Acceptance

Welcome is the first sign of acceptance offered to persons who say that they are spiritually afflicted. When expressing a willingness to listen to these persons, it is necessary, above all, to approach them humbly and respectfully, especially if what they are saying is senseless and apparently the fruit of their imagination. The following are some necessary guidelines.

- Paternally calm the person (bearing in mind that it is easier and quicker to impart a blessing than to condemn).

- Make inquiries with wisdom and prudence, without seeking the sensational or the superstitious. Avoid both a foolish credulity that sees diabolical intervention in every anomaly and difficulty, and a preconceived rationalism that excludes a priori any intervention of the Evil One in the world.

- Warn the person about books, television programs, and news media that exploit the current interest in unusual, extraordinary, or unhealthy phenomena. Urge him never to turn to those who practice magic or who profess to have occult powers, since these persons can be true and proper instruments of the demon and therefore the path to Hell. Where there is doubt about the presence of a diabolical influence, the person must rely solely on the discernment of the exorcist priest and on the support of grace offered by the Church.

• Draw on Sacred Scripture and Tradition to help Christians attain a responsible awareness and a correct attitude toward the presence and action of Satan in the world. Through the *Catechism* and preaching, the priest should instill in them the conviction that superstition, magic, and (even more) Satanism are contrary to the dignity of man and to faith in God the Omnipotent Father and in Jesus Christ, our only Savior.

• Exhort the faithful one to listen attentively and assiduously to the Gospel in order to unmask the Devil's attempt to make us believe that he does not exist. At the same time, urge him to avoid believing that the Evil One is everywhere.

Listening, prayer, and a blessing should never be denied to anyone. To this end there are many possibilities offered by the *Benedictional* of the Church. This willingness on the part of the Church to "be there" can also become a precious opportunity to awaken in the afflicted one a livelier trust in the Risen Christ, more frequent reception of the sacraments, and an increase in participation in the life of the parish.

By increasing their devotion in this way, the faithful afflicted will avoid involvement with the occult. As a result, they will be drawn again to Christ, the Lord of their life and the life of the Church community. The gravity of the suffering of these persons cannot be underestimated:

The Church understands the anxieties, doubts, uncertainties, and suffering of these brothers and sisters, and is committed to assuming — through her ministers — a stance of human assistance and understanding, and an avoidance of every excessive rationalization and cold detachment, whether in the form of fideism or naïve credulousness.[31]

In the presentation of the new *Rite of Exorcism and Prayers for Particular Circumstances*, the Italian Bishops' Conference emphasizes that

the faithful one who asks for an exorcism is someone who that community must love with a preferential love. When he is in the power of the Evil One, he is indeed the poorest of the poor, the neediest of help, understanding, and consolation.[32]

This is the attitude that must animate the Church regarding our brothers and sisters who are vexed or possessed by the Evil One.

---

[31] Conferenza Episcopale Toscana, *A proposito di magia e di demonologia: Nota pastorale* (Rome: Libreria Editrice Vaticana, 1994), p. 3.

[32] Conferenza Episcopale Italiana, *Rito degli esorcismi e preghiere per circostanze particolari* (Rome: Libreria Editrice Vaticana, 2001), p. 13.

14

Discernment: Mental Illness
or Diabolical Attack?

Distinguishing between mental illness and a diabolical attack — two realities with similar manifestations — is a complex and delicate task. For this reason, the priest exorcist must be very diligent in making use of the human sciences of psychiatry and psychology. The enemy is strong when he is hidden, and psychological or psychiatric illnesses are a realm that, in the exorcists' view, is easily infiltrated by him and where he is difficult to discover.

Moreover, there are signs, manifestations, or actions that can vary according to the treatment of one or the other condition. For example, when the person is under attack, his mood can change in a moment. In a few seconds he can go from serene and joyful to irascible and even violent toward things or persons. If, during these irrational mood changes, one prays mentally, invoking the help of Mary or of St. Michael the Archangel, and the person reacts even more violently, then vacillates between moments of calm and raucous anger, we can be certain that we are before a spiritual, not a psychiatric, problem. This occurs mainly in persons who do not have a relationship with Jesus, who do not the practice their Faith. They neither listen to the Gospel, pray, nor receive the sacraments.

Psychological or psychiatric problems, on the contrary, always have an evolution in time and an identifiable cause that is explainable and therefore manageable with suitable medication. In fact, after following the therapy established by a medical doctor, psychological disturbances generally disappear or mitigate.

Once, a person came to me with sudden and unexpected mood changes. Medicine had no effect, and no one was able to explain the cause. She arrived tranquil, but a few seconds after we began the conversation she began to speak angrily. I mentally invoked our Lady, asking her to help me in the discernment. Immediately the person said to me: "Do not call on that one!" It was clear that it was not a psychiatric case.

In the cases of psychiatric or psychological disturbances, there is no reading of the mind or change in the person's behavior when one prays mentally or invokes our Lady, Jesus, or the saints.

It can happen that the enemy is hidden within a family's relational difficulties or is the one causing divisions and hatreds among the relatives. In these cases, it is well for the afflicted to make an act of humility through the sacrament of Reconciliation. For sins committed against relatives (which are also sins against God), he should ask God's pardon. Then he should reconcile with the one he has hated, relying on works of mortification aimed at his arrogance, which generates egotism and pride, which are always latent in our spirit. If we pardon each other reciprocally, the disturbances to our health and our work will quickly disappear and the fulfillment of our life's projects and plans will be restored. Peace will return to our family and to our heart because liberation from an evil action has occurred.

I repeat: in addition to the sacrament of Reconciliation, it is necessary to have the Word of God in one's head, prayer rushing from one's heart, and the Eucharistic encounter with the Risen Jesus.

Among the sudden and more evident signs of attack by the enemy, the most significant are excessive pupil dilation that cannot be altered, not even by shining a direct light on it; the reddening of the sclera, the whites of the eye, as with conjunctivitis (pink eye); the voice becoming raucous and baritone (even if a woman is speaking); the lengthening and darkening of the face; an extraordinary strength beyond the physical possibilities of the person; a violent reaction toward sacred images and objects; the use of unknown languages; and knowledge of the occult.

It happened to me once in the case of a fourteen-year-old girl who, apparently with solely the strength of her will, moved objects and launched them against her grandmother when her grandmother was praying.

Beware! These *powers*, such as reading a person's thoughts and foreseeing the future, *are not natural* and, therefore, do not belong to a human being; otherwise all of us would have them! The mother of this girl, having been deceived by Satan, believed that they were telekinetic capacities that the daughter had been given by a parapsychologist,[33] and therefore I was prevented from praying the exorcism. In this case, the mother also needed prayers.

When unexplainable things happen and medical doctors cannot resolve the problems, do *not* go to sensitives, *alternative medical doctors*, self-styled holders of charisms, wizards, or practitioners of the occult. When someone came to me after having consulted all these persons, not only were the problems unresolved; they were aggravated so much that, as the Gospel says, the condition of that

---

[33] A category that does not exist in traditional medicine. It claims to give scientific explanations for preternatural phenomena.

man was worse than before. In these cases, it is always necessary, above all, for the afflicted person first to go to Confession and receive Holy Communion. Then he must go to his pastor (or to any priest) for a prayer of liberation. If then, after repeated prayers, there is no improvement, it is necessary to consult the priest exorcist of the person's diocese.

15

Instruments of
Discernment and Help

Fidelity to Baptism

The Devil tries to undermine the spiritual reality that was given to each of us through the sacrament of Baptism: the dignity and mission that make us children of God and cancel the sin of pride (original sin) that tarnished human nature and the will of man. With Baptism, Jesus gives us the possibility of returning to the image and likeness of God, which among all the created beings belongs solely to man. Not even the Angel of Light has it.

Man, having the capacity of free will and will, can overcome the laws of nature and, through Baptism, with the help of God, can freely make the right choices. It is necessary, then, to be faithful to our Baptism in our way of thinking and acting and in our obedience to God's teachings.

During His earthly life Jesus exemplifies the life of man as the image and likeness of God. Some characteristics of the new man generated through Baptism are humility, simplicity, the capacity to love and to pardon, and total trust in and obedience to the Creator. The enemy continuously attempts to turn us against God and neighbor and pushes us to betray our baptismal promises (it would be beautiful and helpful to our soul if every now and then we would repeat the renunciations of Satan and pray the Creed).

Even the saints were tempted, some severely. But consistency and fidelity to their Baptism made them victorious over the actions of Satan. And each day of our earthly lives, without respite or reprieve, we also engage in a difficult spiritual struggle in our choices, actions, and comportment. It is necessary, then, continuously to compare our thoughts, feelings, and actions with those of Jesus, so that we can learn through repeated listening to the Gospel that only by having the Word of God in our consciousness will we be able to defend the identity and dignity of our Baptism and our human and spiritual life.

In conclusion, infidelity to our Baptism becomes the springboard for the extraordinary action of the Devil. In fact, sin is the fissure through which the Devil is able to penetrate and touch our lives. By sinning, we give permission to Satan to influence our choices and our lives. Then, rather than God, the ego takes over. Arrogance sets aside humility and generates pride and egoism. Thus, the quality of our human and spiritual life is strictly connected to Baptism and conversion.

Prayer – Ordinary, Evocative, and Intercessory

Prayer is the way we converse with God. We must reject the notion that prayer is a religious practice enclosed in a series of things to say or do, or that it is the fruit of our own initiative. On this matter Jesus' teaching helps us:

> And when you pray, you must not be like the hypocrites; for they love to stand and pray in the synagogues and at the street corners, that they may be seen by men. Truly, I say to you, they have their reward. But when you pray, go

into your room and shut the door and pray to your Father who is in secret; and your Father who sees in secret will reward you.

And in praying do not heap up empty phrases as the Gentiles do; for they think that they will be heard for their many words. Do not be like them, for your Father knows what you need before you ask him. Pray then like this:

Our Father who art in heaven,

Hallowed be thy name.

Thy kingdom come,

Thy will be done,

On earth as it is in heaven.

Give us this day our daily bread;

And forgive us our debts,

As we also have forgiven our debtors;

And lead us not into temptation,

But deliver us from evil.

For if you forgive men their trespasses, your heavenly Father also will forgive you; but if you do not forgive men their trespasses, neither will your Father forgive your trespasses. (Matt. 6:5–15)

Jesus points out that conversation with God the Father must be free of superfluous words and hypocritical attitudes. The substance and efficacy of prayer to God is confidence in the certainty of its being heard.

In teaching the Lord's Prayer, Jesus makes an important synthesis of all that is essential to be listened to and responded to by God the Father. In the seven petitions contained in this prayer we find a true and proper lifestyle, which culminates with the supplication and request to be protected and liberated from evil.

There exists, however, an absolute condition without which it is not granted: the pardon. In all His life Jesus teaches us that there is no love if there is no pardon. It is fundamental to understand this because it is what counteracts the action of Satan, which is the exposition of hate and wickedness.

Prayer, more than a series of personal requests, must be a conversation in loving communion with God the Father and with the Son, who is the teacher, guide, and gate of access to the heart of God and neighbor.

Prayer is a help and accompaniment in the encounter with evil spirits, but it is also an instrument of discernment that invokes the intervention of Jesus, Mary, and the saints. This invocation unmasks the extraordinary action of the Devil, who in his pride cannot resist being hunted. It is not our prayer that drives away the Devil, but the invoked intervention of Jesus and Mary.

Prayer must not lose its fundamental characteristics, or it loses its efficacy. It must

- come forth from a heart in the state of grace, through frequent reception of the sacraments of Reconciliation and the Eucharist
- be rooted in total trust and abandonment in Jesus, Mary, and the saints
- manifest communion with the Church
- have a precise spiritual intention

Prayer for a precise intention has the character of intercessory prayer. In this sphere let us emphasize how important it is not to fall into the error of offering oneself or one's life in order to intercede on behalf of another. In this case, one is dangerously exposed to the direct action of the Evil One. Only Jesus, Mary, and the saints can intercede in favor of the person or the deceased for whom we ask intercession. We cannot clash or go to combat directly with the Evil One, since we are human beings, inferior to him. Satan is an angel, a spiritual person, preternatural, superior to human nature, but he is not of the same spirituality as God, who is supernatural. In the prayer of intercession, we can only entrust to God the person for whom we are praying. Jesus assured us: "Whatever you ask in my name, I will do it, that the Father may be glorified in the Son" (John 14:13), so entrusting the prayer of intercession to Him will make it efficacious.

The Prayer of Liberation

Another efficacious prayer is the prayer of liberation, so named for its intention. It is a prayer of invocation to God the Father for His mercy and to the Holy Spirit for a grace in favor of the person for whom one is praying. Anyone can pray a prayer of liberation from evil for himself or for others. As with any prayer, the formulation can be varied, as long as it maintains the characteristic of invocation and supplication.

Above all, *the prayer of liberation must never give a direct command to the Devil.* If, at the center of the prayer of liberation, there is a direct command, we find ourselves saying a prayer of exorcism. Whoever prays a prayer of exorcism, other than a priest authorized by the bishop of the diocese, risks the extraordinary direct action of the Devil on himself. In fact, the Evil One interprets this prayer as a haughty challenge from a creature whom he considers inferior to himself. Exorcists can confirm that a prayer of liberation that contains a direct command, prayed by laymen in a private forum for themselves or for others, can be the cause of extraordinary spiritual disturbances on the part of the Devil. We exorcists suggest that persons in need of a prayer of liberation turn only to a priest, who will pronounce this prayer on the interested person.

It is important to remember that, in Jesus' own words—"where two or three are gathered in my name, there am I in the midst of them" (Matt. 18:20)—prayer becomes particularly efficacious when it is expressed in unity by persons with the same intention, praying in His name.

The Prayer of Exorcism

In the struggle against Satan, the Church accompanies the faithful with prayer and invocation of the efficacious presence of Christ, through the faith and through the words of Jesus:

> And I tell you, you are Peter, and on this rock I will build my church, and the powers of death shall not prevail against it. I will give you the keys of the kingdom of heaven, and whatever you bind on earth shall be bound in heaven, and whatever you loose on earth shall be loosed in heaven. (Matt. 16:18–19).

This is the ordinary pastoral tradition of the Church with the rite of exorcism in the celebration of Baptism.[34] In foreseen cases, it is done in a specific way with the sacramental prayer of exorcism, through which one asks the Lord for victory over Satan. In the *Catechism*, we find the definition of the prayer of exorcism:

> When the Church asks publicly and authoritatively in the name of Jesus Christ that a person or object be protected against the power of the Evil One and withdrawn from his dominion, it is called exorcism. Jesus performed exorcisms

---

[34] Cf. Conferenza Episcopale Italiana, *Rito del Battesimo* (Rome: Libreria Editrice Vaticana, 1995), nos. 104–105.

and from him the Church has received the power and office of exorcizing (see Mark 1:25–26; 3:15; 6:7, 13; 16:17). In a simple form, exorcism is performed at the celebration of Baptism. The solemn exorcism, called "a major exorcism," can be performed only by a priest and with the permission of the bishop. The priest must proceed with prudence, strictly observing the rules established by the Church. Exorcism is directed at the expulsion of demons or to the liberation from demonic possession through the spiritual authority which Jesus entrusted to his Church. (no. 1673)

The prayer of exorcism must be utilized, as established by the Church, solely in the case of a verified demonic possession,[35] a discernment that is entrusted exclusively to the exorcist priest authorized by the diocesan bishop. Such a prayer must be offered in private and must avoid every appearance of theatrical display or exploitation. Videotaping, filming, or recording the exorcist ritual is strictly forbidden, as established by the norms of the same rite in the *Praenotanda* (*Rite of Exorcism*):[36]

> Exorcism must be carried out in a way that manifests the faith of the Church and prevents it from being interpreted as an act of magic or superstition. One must avoid turning it into a spectacle for those present. During the course of the exorcism, all methods of production related to recording or videotaping are forbidden, both before and after

---

[35] See Congregation for Divine Worship and the Discipline of the Sacraments, *De exorcismis et supplicationibus quibusdam* (Rome: Libreria Editrice Vaticana, 2001), nos. 16 and 17.

[36] See ibid., no. 19.

the rite, so that both the exorcist and those present avoid vulgarizing the ritual, maintaining a proper reserve.[37]

Let us recall that, according to the *Rite*, the gestures permitted during the celebration of the exorcism are: the Sign of the Cross, the imposition of the hands (by the exorcist) only on the head, insufflation (breathing on the person), aspersion (sprinkling) of blessed water, and the ostension (showing) of the crucifix. The exorcist must be particularly attentive to his own actions during this extremely delicate and important ministry. He must avoid remaining alone with the tormented person and, while with him, must avoid everything—expressions, deeds, and tones—that could stir up agitation or inspire misunderstandings. Above all, he must avoid gestures that could generate suspicions about his own virtue and character.

Moreover, the exorcist must never forget that the struggle against the demon occurs on a spiritual, not a physical, level. Therefore, if at times during the exorcism it is necessary to intervene in order to block the violent and aggressive movements that the tormented person may manifest, he must avoid harming him and those assisting or accompanying him. Also, the exorcist must avoid using bullying tactics or attitudes as a way of combating and humiliating the demon.

Exorcist priests must remember that the efficacy of the prayer of liberation is subordinated to respect for the norms established by the Church and in obedience to the appropriate diocesan bishop.

All the prayers must be expressions of a heart in communion with Jesus and with the faith and intentions of His Church. Furthermore, both the tormented faithful and the priest exorcist

---

[37] Conferenza Episcopale Italiana, *Rito degli esorcismi*, p. 19.

are exhorted to entrust themselves to the Faith and the grace of God obtained through the sacraments of Reconciliation and the Eucharist.[38]

Let us reaffirm the Church's rule regarding the protection of the one who is authorized to pray the exorcism: this prayer can be repeated solely by a priest who has been given a written license from his bishop. This license protects the exorcist from the extraordinary action of the Devil upon him, since he is acting in obedience to the Church.

It is, then, right to advise and exhort everyone to keep his distance from improvised exorcists, both laymen and priests. *Some laymen say they have permission from the bishop. This is false!*

The exorcist of the diocese is the bishop, or a priest designated by the bishop expressly for this purpose. The priest must have a written license from the bishop himself, or he cannot practice the ministry of exorcism, nor can other priests. We must also be aware of self-styled holders of charisms, wizards, or practitioners of the occult, who are in reality mediums or sensitives. Let us not be deceived by their display of statues, sacred images, or prayers in the places where they receive their followers. These things do not at all certify faith in God; rather, they are there as items of deceit that cover up service to the forces of the Evil One. These persons are voluntarily or involuntarily deceived by the Evil One into believing they possess powers or faculties that are beneficial to their neighbor. If these powers were natural, everyone would have them. If a person has gifts from God, these must be certified and validated by the Church; that is, by the diocesan bishop in his role as the local pastor.

---

[38] See Pio XII, *Titulus XII*, "De Exorcizandis Obsessis a Daemonio," *Ritualis Romani*, Editio typica, 1952, chap. 2, no. 1.

Further discussion

About prayer, it is necessary to make an additional clarification regarding its efficacy in cases of the extraordinary action of the Devil. Some may think that through particular prayers or blessings that make use of specific formulations and sacramentals (such as water, salt, and blessed oil), the efficacy is greater and the liberation more immediate. In fact, this type of credence, or thought, manifests a magical and superstitious attitude that has nothing to do with the Christian faith. Furthermore, it is clearly in contrast with what Jesus teaches about a humble and confident attitude toward God's intervention. In fact, this type of logic or religious philosophy expresses a self-determination, individualism, or independence that leads a person to believe that he can do it alone. This is a fruit of the modern culture that accentuates materialism as the source of one's security and personal capacities.

The efficacy of the prayer is not ever determined by the way it is recited or by the words pronounced. (This does happen with magical formulas, where it is necessary to describe the thing that is asked for from the Devil.)

The efficacy of a prayer of exorcism is directly related to the petitioner's trust in God. Prayer that successfully chases or distances the Evil One will not have any particular characteristic; rather, it must be expressed with total confidence in the intervention of Jesus, Mary, and the saints.

16

When and How to Ask for Help

When to approach an exorcist priest

After having had a discussion to determine whether the person is facing one of the situations cited above, the priest—usually the pastor—begins a prayer of supplication for discernment so that he may come to know if the person needs to turn to an exorcist.

The priest can begin by inviting the person to pray. Meanwhile, he asks repeatedly that God's blessings descend on him, invoking the Holy Spirit and the intercession of Mary.

The Lord's Prayer, the Hail Mary, the prayer to St. Michael the Archangel, and a request for intercession by the saints are efficacious prayers. If the priest notes some reactions, he can proceed to the prayer of invocation and, after some minutes, conclude with the blessing. These periods of prayer are repeated on three days. Each time, the priest notes the behavior and reactions of the person for whom he is praying.

In the reactions of the possibly afflicted one, the priest must be alert for movements of the head, the inability to support the weight of the priest's hand on his head, belching and continuous coughing, vomiting, overheating, a burning sensation or cold chills, feelings of electric shocks on the body, acute pains, upset stomach, a sense of suffocation, the desire to interrupt the prayer and flee, feeling faint, and other such phenomena. If any such reactions occur in the three successive days of blessings, the priest must send the afflicted one to the exorcist.

If the person complains of apathy, tends toward depression, or experiences protracted physical pains without explanation, it is necessary to seek medical help. If there is no medical solution, then it is advisable to begin a verification in prayer. If, on the other hand, there have been no particular reactions on the part of the person, and he feels serene and content, then there is not any diabolical presence.

It can happen that even from the first blessing, or in a successive one, the person, at least apparently, manifests a harmful presence. In general, signs that can indicate the evil action are that the faithful seems to change personality, feeling a great oppression associated with the refusal of sacred things, words, or places, and exhibits a hatred toward God, the Madonna, and the saints, to the point of becoming furious and aggressive (even if it is contrary to the person's nature), or suddenly exhibits great physical strength accompanied by yelling, spitting, and drooling. At the same time, one may observe a change in the voice timbre and facial expression. A new personality may emerge, expressing an implacable hatred toward a victim, threatening his spiritual and physical destruction. During this display, the afflicted one's eyes can be sealed and, if at some moments they are opened, the pupils appear completely or nearly completely turned around in the eye socket (without blinking) and the pupils are dilated. The entity then manifested may demonstrate knowledge of things that the person cannot know, such as speaking languages unknown to him or revealing knowledge of persons around him or deeds that will happen in the distant future. These phenomena can correspond to a diabolical possession; therefore, when a priest observes these signs, he should contact the exorcist so that the faithful can be presented for his discernment.

In the ordinary life of a person, certain signs can indicate an extraordinary diabolical action: in some cases, the person may have physical symptoms or illnesses that medications and various cures cannot resolve; relationships that are broken off without explanation and without valid motives; sudden and unmotivated job losses or continuous obstacles to work; sleep disturbances, including monstrous dreams or nightmares, or sudden reawakenings, usually between one and four in the morning. At times these persons speak of waking up tired, notwithstanding many hours of rest; or they find bruises, marks, wounds, and scratches on their body. They may report waking up in pain, as if they had been hit, or have migraines. They may experience sudden apathies, depressive thoughts, or feel that somehow time itself has slowed down.

Still other persons tell of perceiving noises or odors (sulfur, rottenness, burnt items, smoke, and excrement), or both, see shadows or presences around them, or feel intense bodily or atmospheric cold in an ambience that is heated. Other symptoms are states of unmotivated nervousness, violent and visceral feelings toward things and persons, irritability, sudden and unmotivated changes of mood, rejection and hatred toward the sacred and prayers, or brief losses of memory caused by a state of trance. All these behaviors reveal either the possible presence of the extraordinary action of the demon, a psychic imbalance, or both. In order for the exorcist priest to make an adequate and prudent evaluation of the causes of the person's malaise, he will have to avail himself of the help of specialists in the field of psychology and psychiatry.

How to accompany and sustain the afflicted

There are several ways a priest or a relative can help the person with probable spiritual disturbances.

Above all, it is necessary to examine the life of faith of the afflicted person. Does he live a relationship of trust in and love toward Jesus? This is verifiable by looking at how he lives the commandments, either as life teachings or as rules more or less transgressed. In particular, it is important to put God at the center of his daily life so that his choices, sentiments, thoughts, and behaviors may be examined in the light of the teachings of the Gospel. If his communion with God has been interrupted by sin, it is important that he ask pardon as often as necessary in the sacrament of Reconciliation. Then he must sanctify Sundays and feast days by participating at Holy Mass. And he must daily dedicate some moments to prayer (such as the Rosary, Eucharistic adoration, and so forth).

A powerful and at times decisive help is the union in prayer of the family of the person in difficulty. The Rosary prayed together, the Gospel proclaimed and shared in the home, invocation of the Holy Spirit and the profession of faith (the Creed) prayed by all the family members together, reconciled and communicating, often brings relief to the suffering person and at times even achieves total and lasting liberation.

Consideration must also be given to the characteristics of the disturbances: how they are manifested, for how long, how they have been developing, whether one remembers an initial cause and a reaction, the remedies used, the diagnoses and medical cures that followed, whether they were accompanied by reactions to sacred items or circumstances, whether the reactions were violent or nonviolent, and what were the opinions of qualified persons.

It is fundamental to emphasize that whenever a priest or a family member finds himself before a sudden violent and aggressive crisis, he must never react with the same type of violence or repressive behavior. He must always maintain control and avoid falling into the provocations and insults that demons manifest toward the tormented person. Rather, He must work in this way:

- Try to limit or block the person's movements without restraining him physically, so that no harm is done to him or to those present.
- If possible, try to lay him down.
- Pray mentally with the intention of invoking the intervention of Jesus, Mary, St. Michael the Archangel, and all the saints.
- Make an act of faith, marking the Sign of the Cross on the person's forehead, invoking the name of Jesus (saying: "In the Name of Jesus"), using, if present, blessed water. In this context it is useful to pray mentally with faith, in order to discover whether there is an extraordinary diabolical presence.

If, following mental prayer, there is a reaction of calm or further violence, it is necessary to call the exorcist priest, since only the Devil can know that in that moment someone was praying.

One must avoid falling into a superstitious mentality that considers a series of controversies the result of a spell or the evil eye, attributes liberating powers to the use of certain objects, or, even worse, imparts direct orders to the demon (at the risk of one's own life!).

The pastoral action of the priest

The first phase of the pastoral action consists in lovingly *calming and accompanying* (fear renders the person fragile and vulnerable).

The apostle Paul tells us: "For you did not receive the spirit of slavery to fall back into fear, but you have received the spirit of sonship. When we cry, 'Abba! Father!'" (Rom. 8:15). We have God for a Father. We have in Christ the certainty of salvation and protection! We have in the Virgin Mary a Mother who loves us immensely, who listens to us, understands us, and is next to us as no other mother can be. Let us bring everyone to the arms of this Mother and encourage them to have great confidence in her whose heart is our true well-being, more than we ourselves are able to desire and wish. Moreover, we must invoke the help of the archangel St. Michael, the guardian angels, and all the saints, who give great certainty of victory in tribulations and hope for a rapid liberation.

The second phase of pastoral action requires a *continuous and sustained vigilance*. According to the warning of the apostle Peter: "Be sober, be watchful. Your adversary the devil prowls around like a roaring lion, seeking some one to devour. Resist him, firm in your faith" (1 Pet. 5:8–9).

Vigilance must be exercised, above all, in regard to the ordinary action of Satan (temptation), with which he continues to tempt men to evil. Temptation is the most serious and dangerous peril since it is directly opposed to God's salvific design and the edification of the Kingdom. Therefore, in order not to stumble, the believer must keep watch and pray each day with the words suggested by Jesus: "Father, do not put us to the test, but save us from the Evil One" (see Matt. 6:13).

Although the extraordinary diabolical phenomena of possession, obsession, vexation, and infestation are possible, and although they provoke great sufferings, by themselves they cannot distance a person from God, and they do not bear the gravity of sin.

It would be foolish, then, to pay too much attention to the presence of the Evil One in some unusual phenomena and not be concerned at all with the daily reality of temptation and sin, in which Satan, the killer from the beginning and the father of lies, is continuously at work (see John 8:44). Vigilance about daily temptations is grounded in three strong foundations:

The Word, and in constant, meditative listening to it

The Gospel and Sacred scripture are excellent defensive and offensive weapons against the demon. Jesus gives us an example of this in His temptations in the desert (see Luke. 4:1–13). It is also necessary to reaffirm fidelity to our Baptism, which connects us to God, the One to whom we must orient our life. Jesus must guide every step, thought, sentiment, and action of our existence.

Prayer

A truly Christian life is sustained by listening to the Word of God and by incessant prayers of thanksgiving and trust. The Psalms are very useful prayers, as are, in general, all the common Christian prayers based on Sacred Scripture. Also recommended are prayers for the use of the faithful in the struggle against the powers of darkness, found in the appendix of the new *Rite of Exorcism*; for example:

> God of mercy and source of every good, you have wished that your Son submit for us to the torture of the cross, in order to liberate us from the power of our mortal enemy. Look with benevolence on my humiliation and my pain: you who in the baptismal font have made me a new creature, help me conquer the Evil One and fill me again

with the grace of your benediction, through Christ our Lord. Amen.[39]

It is also necessary to foster moments of personal and communal prayer in the parish, in particular in Eucharistic adoration, the Rosary, and the Stations of the Cross.

The sacraments

Listening to the Word of God and the prayerful responses prepare the faithful for *the encounter with God in the sacraments*. These can be understood by reading the *Catechism of the Catholic Church* in its first edition. Clear catechesis about the sacrament of Reconciliation is fundamental to living according to the humble example of Christ. Genuine Christian life is indeed a faithful abandonment to the paternal and provident love of God (see Luke 12:22–31) and obedience to His will (see Matt. 6:10).

It is necessary to urge on the afflicted the regular reception of the sacrament of Confession, prepared in advance with a thorough examination of conscience, the forgiving enemies, and prayers that the Lord's illumination may show them the confusion into which they have fallen. This Christian charity is both a duty and a protection from the effects of practicing the occult. The invitation to the life of prayer should consist, above all, in participation in the Holy Sacrifice of the Mass each Sunday and, when possible, even daily. Moments of adoration of the Most Holy Sacrament, praying the Rosary, acts of devotion to our Lady, and meditating on the Passion help us to recall Jesus' humility on the Cross and His victory over evil and death. It is

---

[39] Conferenza Episcopale Italiana, *Rito degli esorcismi*, Appendix 2, no. 4.

also advisable, from time to time, to invoke with heartfelt faith the name of Jesus (see Acts 4:12) and of the Virgin Mary. Listening to the Word of God, praying, and receiving the sacraments must be components of a Christian's daily life.

The third phase of pastoral action is *the faithful's active insertion into parish life*. With Baptism, the Christian becomes part of the *family of God*, the "summoned," the Church (*ecclesia*). This belonging is nurtured through communal listening and personal meditation on the Word of God, frequent participation in the Mass, and the sacrament of Reconciliation. Confession of sins is necessary in order to obtain pardon from God and to return refreshed to the community of the children of God. We also receive further support from the other sacraments. To live and participate in the life of the community makes us feel like a part of a reality greater than the one in which we are living. Sacramental communion is accomplished through the fraternal and prayerful communion with the Christian community and it is based on that first community gathered around Jesus. Offering service to the community is an expression of love toward the needy and toward the same Christian community.

All priests, exorcist and nonexorcist, are urged *not to lose spiritual sight of the persons who are victims* of the extraordinary attacks of the demon. We must try to accompany them in their spiritual journey toward Jesus, helping them where they are deficient: in their knowledge of catechesis, in their doubts about their faith, in being lax in prayer and in the reception of the sacraments, so that what Jesus says may not happen:

> When the unclean spirit has gone out of a man, he passes through waterless places seeking rest; and finding none he says, "I will return to my house from which I came." And

when he comes he finds it swept and put in order. Then he goes and brings seven other spirits more evil than himself, and they enter and dwell there; and the last state of that man becomes worse than the first. (Luke 11:24–26)

The disciple of Christ overcomes difficulties and fulfills honest desires by uniting his faith in God to provident and responsible projects, opportunely supporting and enhancing his activities through the use of scientific and technological progress. He knows that Christian faith is incompatible with superstition, magic, and Satanism; rather, it is the best ally of man's responsible commitment.

Conclusion

In spite of all that has been covered in this treatise, I must emphasize that I have not exhausted this topic, which is vast and complex. My intention is to provide a little help to priests and laity who may find themselves before persons with apparent spiritual disturbances that, if they prove genuine, need help and accompaniment.

Today, more than ever, we are combating ideologies and a personal morality that rejects absolute objective criteria. The provoker of all this is the one whom Paul VI defined as "the perverse and the perverter," a personal spiritual reality who is really present and active. The action of the Evil One is obvious in the origins of logic and behavior that leads to the refusal of God, solely for one's personal gain and self-adoration. The principal way of combating him is to stay away from his activity. He is a dog tied to a chain: he is not omnipotent. Maintaining a relationship with God through the Gospel and through prayer and the sacraments serves to keep him tied. On the other hand, our sins lengthen the chain and permit him to ruin us.

God Himself comes to meet us by incarnating Himself in the person of Jesus, permitting us to listen and dialogue with God Himself and enabling us to distance ourselves from the cruel enemy.

In this text I have tried to furnish some instruments that help us recognize the temptations and the extraordinary actions of the Devil in our daily life. Aspirations, projects, and desires that are legitimate in this earthly life can, because of the tempting and, at times, extraordinary action of the Devil, become enslavement when they exalt arrogance, pride, and egoism. This happens when the Word of God does not guide our choices and, in general, together with a weakened faith, there is no other way to verify the absolute truth of such choices.

In this text I have also attempted to illustrate the instruments that Jesus Himself has given to us in order to combat temptations and liberate us from the extraordinary action of the Evil One: the Gospel, prayer, and the sacraments. They are the three feet of the table of our human and spiritual life that are necessary to keep it tidy and serene for eternal life. We have also seen how necessary it is to be vigilant regarding both places and persons who may involve us in spiritually dangerous situations. God's commandments and the Word of God help us in this vigilance. It is important not to fall into self-isolation or live an isolated individualistic dimension of prayer. Prayer itself acquires more strength if it comes from a community of persons united in the name of Jesus in the Faith and in the only God. It is important that the community be guided by a shepherd attentive to the spiritual life of the souls entrusted to him, and by priests who guide and stimulate a life of faith and prayer through correct liturgical celebrations and a clear catechesis that is faithful to the Magisterium of the Church.

God, the Almighty Father, does not permit the demon to take us.

Jesus came to be our guide and our teacher and to show us that rejecting the Devil drives him away. In Mary, the most holy one, the Mother of the Lord, our Mother, and the Mother of the Church, we have a powerful protector and an infallible example of humility and fidelity to the only God. Moreover, we have St. Michael the Archangel and our guardian angel, who continuously protect us from the assaults of the enemy.

To us is left the steady and attentive vigilance of not allowing temptation to become sin. This is the door through which the demon enters our life, influencing our choices and our behavior. The life of man subsists in the vision of God. St. Irenaeus of Lyons affirms it:

> Those who see God will receive life because the splendor of God is lifegiving. And although He is boundless, beyond comprehension, and invisible, He makes Himself visible and comprehensible … to those who believe, so that He might enliven those who receive Him and behold Him through faith. For indeed as His greatness is beyond understanding, so also is His goodness beyond expression. But through these—His greatness and His goodness—He reveals Himself and bestows life upon those who see Him.
>
> It is not possible to live without life, and life consists in fellowship with God, which is seeing God and enjoying His goodness.… And He who works all things in all is God, but His nature and greatness are invisible and remain invisible to all who have been made by Him.… Yet He is by no means unknown because through the Word, all arrive at the knowledge of the One Father who contains all things, and gives existence to all things. As the Gospel also says: "No one has ever seen God; it is only the Son, who is close to the Father's heart, who has made Him known" (John 1:18).

Therefore, from the beginning, the Son is the revealer of the Father, inasmuch as he was with the Father from the beginning. Also from the beginning the Son has shown man ... visions and a diversity of gifts (charisms), his own ministrations, and the glory of the Father. And he has composed for man a harmonious melody for man's utility so that he may impede man from ceasing to exist. Indeed, the glory of God is the living man, and the life of man consists in the vision of God. If God's revelation already gives life to all beings on earth, how much more is the manifestation of the Father through the Word the cause of life for those who see God.[40]

For the glory and honor of the Most Holy Trinity, let us live our life as an offering pleasing to God and for eternal life. Amen. Peace and goodness!

[40] Irenaeus of Lyons, *Against Heresies* 4:20, 5–7.

Appendices

Appendix I

A Practical Outline for the Priest

How to receive the person

- Listen seriously, and paternally calm the faithful (it is easier and swifter to impart a blessing than to persuade).
- With wisdom and prudence, ask the faithful not to seek the sensational and to avoid both foolish credulity (which sees diabolical intervention in each anomaly and difficulty) and a preconceived rationalism that excludes a priori every form of intervention of the Evil One in the world.
- Make the faithful wary of books, television programs, and means of communication whose objective is to exploit others for profit by awakening widespread interest in unusual and unhealthy phenomena.
- Exhort the faithful to beware of those who practice magic or claim to possess occult powers and those who are mediumistic or presume to have received particular powers, because these are true and proper instruments of the demon and paths to Hell. When in doubt about the presence of diabolical influence, rely solely on the discernment of the exorcist priest and the support of grace offered by the Church, above all in the sacraments.
- Explain the authentic meaning of the language used by Sacred Scripture and Tradition, and teach the Christians

how to acquire a correct attitude toward the presence and action of Satan in the world.

• In preaching, citing the *Catechism of the Catholic Church*, remind the faithful that superstition, magic and, even more so, Satanism, are contrary to man's dignity, rationality, and faith in God.

• Unmask the deceit by means of which the demon tries to make us believe that he does not exist.

• Listening and, as much as possible, prayer followed by a blessing from one's pastor should not be denied to anyone. There are many prayerful examples in the *Benedictional* promulgated by the Church.

Listening and discernment

1. It is necessary to determine the level of the life of faith of the person suffering.

Specifically:

• whether he lives God's commandments
• whether he confesses his sins frequently
• whether he participates at Holy Mass
• whether he prays (the Rosary, adoration of the Eucharist, the Stations of the Cross, and so forth)

2. It is necessary to determine the type of disturbances:

• how they are manifested
• how long they have lasted
• how they developed
• whether the initial cause can be recalled
• whether the person has had reactions, violent or nonviolent, toward sacred things
• what qualified persons have said

Causes of spiritual disturbances and when to approach an exorcist

The possible cause of spiritual disturbances can be:

* participation in spiritualist séances or having assisted at them
* consulting wizards, psychics, or mediums or personally engaging in such activities
* making use of amulets, charms, and talismans, above all if they were received from wizards
* returning from trips abroad with souvenirs of the local magic, or assisting at rituals of the local magic
* practicing certain techniques related to the New Age movement or having attended séances to receive potions that supposedly dispel illnesses (magical cures)
* having been a part of sects, groups, or associations in which esoteric rites were carried out, pseudo-spiritual or pseudo-charismatic
* having taken part in or joined a satanic sect or having taken part in satanic rites, such as blood pacts made with demons; having participated in black masses and the voluntary profanation of the Eucharist
* having engaged in or witnessed ritual homicides
* having listened for long periods of time and many hours a day to music with messages that are invitations to satanic cults or to violence, necrophilia, blasphemy, homicides, or suicides; having participated in so-called alternative religious movements

It is also important to discover:

* whether the person has been subjected to traumatic experiences (physical or sexual violence, assaults, injuries, etc.)

* whether the person has serious sins that have never been confessed (e.g., abortion) or for which he has made insufficient reparation
* whether the person has committed grave injustices that have not been remedied, sustained hatreds that have not been expunged, refused to pardon others, and so forth

Discernment in prayer

* Find out whether the person has been involved in one of the situations alluded to above.
* Begin by inviting the person to pray, while the priest prays in a repetitive way for God's blessing, for the Holy Spirit, and for the protection of Mary to descend on the person. If reactions are noted, the priest then proceeds with the prayer of invocation and trust and concludes with the blessing.
* Discover whether there have been any strange reactions or sensations in the person, such as head spinning, feeling the priest's hand on the head to be insupportable, continuous belching and coughing, vomiting, feverish heat or cold chills, sensations like electric shocks on the body, acute pains, upset stomach, nausea, a sense of suffocation, the desire to interrupt prayer and flee, or feeling faint. If these phenomena are repeated in successive blessings, it is necessary to approach an exorcist.
* If the person feels well but was prostrated, as if he were very tired, it would be good to do subsequent determinations, prayers, and blessings to ascertain whether there is some hidden evil presence too strong to resist. In such cases, it is necessary to approach an exorcist.

• If there are no particular reactions on the part of the person and he feels serene and content, there is no diabolical presence.

Possible manifestations of the extraordinary action of Satan

• The person seems to change personality and feels a sense of great oppression, rejecting sacred things, words, or sacred places (hatred toward God, our Lady, and the saints), even to becoming furious and aggressive, unleashing great physical strength with screams, spitting, and slavering.

• The person manifests a change in the timbre of his voice or facial distortions.

• A new personality emerges and demonstrates implacable hatred toward his victim, threatening his physical and spiritual destruction.

• The person's eyes either close completely, as if sealed or, if opened, the pupils appear completely or nearly completely turned toward the orbital cavity or appear for a certain time completely wide open without batting an eyelid.

• The person has knowledge of things he should not be able to know, such as languages unknown to him or secret facts about persons around him or facts that happened in the past.

How you should accompany the afflicted

• Always bear yourself with charity, patience, attention, and respect toward what the afflicted person is saying.

- Urge and accompany the afflicted one with continuous and meditative listening to the Word of God, to overcome the temptations and attacks of the Evil One and as a way of thinking, loving, and acting like Jesus.
- Invite and join the person in ceaseless prayers of gratitude and trust.
- Renew fidelity to your own Baptism in living a life in conformity with the teachings of Jesus.
- Find a place and time each day to live the encounter with Jesus through prayerful meditation on the Word of God and with our Lady in the Rosary.
- Find time for communal prayer in the parish through adoration of the Most Holy Sacrament, and by praying the Rosary and the Stations of the Cross.
- Deepen your encounter with God in the sacraments through a good catechesis.
- Make an act of devotion daily to our Lady and frequently pronounce invocations prayed with faith in the name of Jesus and of the Virgin Mary.
- Encourage an active involvement of the afflicted person in parish life.

Prayers for the One Attacked and for the Priest Who Accompanies Him

To God, our only hope

O God,
the only hope of the world,
the only refuge for unhappy man,
abiding in the faithfulness of Heaven,
give me true help in this difficult battle.
O great King, save Your servant from defeat:
lest weak flesh succumb to the terrible Tyrant,
facing innumerable blows alone.
Remember I am dust and wind and shadow,
and my life is as fleeting as the flowering of the grass:
but may Your mercy,
resplendent from all eternity,
rescue Thy servant from the jaws of the lion.
Thou who didst come from on high in the cloak of
    flesh,
strike down the Dragon with the two-edged sword,
enabling our mortal flesh to war with winds and beat
    down strongholds (evil spirits)

with our Captain God.
If battles rage,
if the slimy snake cries out,
if the ferocious enemy incites his own to war,
under your guidance, victory is assured.
Holding fast to you no terrible serpent can upset us.
Liberate me, O Most High,
from infernal traps
so that I may approach the true light, O great King,
and, flourishing in the splendor of your temple,
take part in Heaven's sacred chorus.

—Venerable St. Bede[41]

Mary, liberate me and save me

O most Holy Sovereign Queen, O Mother of God, with
the help of your saints and through your powerful prayers,
keep me away from me all discouragement, lukewarm-
ness, laziness, error, and every impure, bad, and evil
thought coming from my miserable heart and darkened
intelligence.

Extinguish the flame of my passions, I who am poor
and miserable. Liberate me from my many and bad memo-
ries and actions, and preserve me from every bad deed.

Because you are blessed among all peoples and your
name venerated and glorified forever and ever. Amen.

—Macario the Egyptian

[41] *Hymni; Patrologia Latina, suppl.* IV, 2237.

To Mary

O you, who in the continuous uncertainty
of the present life are jostled by storms,
without a secure place to find support, lean on Mary.

Keep your glance fixed on the splendor of this star
if you do not wish to be swept away by the storms.
When the winds of temptation rise
and you go to battle against tribulations,
look at the star, invoke Mary!

If the swells of pride, ambition,
calumny, and envy
thrust you here and there,
look at the star, invoke Mary!

If anger, avarice, and hedonism
toss the little boat of your soul,
turn your thoughts to Mary.

If you are troubled by the enormity of your sins,
mortified by shameful things on your conscience,
frightened at the terrible thought of judgment,
and if you are about to dive into the abyss of desperation,
think of Mary!

In dangers, distress, and perplexities,
think of Mary, invoke Mary!

Let Mary be always on your lips and in your heart.
And to obtain her intercession, follow her example.
If you follow her, you will not get lost.
If you pray to her, you will not lose hope.

If you think of her, you will not err.
Sustained by her, you will not fall.
Defended by her, you will not fear.
With her guidance, you will not tire.
With her benevolence, you will reach your destination.
Amen.

—St. Bernard of Clairvaux

Prayer of our Holy Father
John Paul II to Our Lady of Divine Love

Hail, O Mother, Queen of the world.
You are the Mother of fair Love.
You are the Mother of Jesus,
the source of all grace,
the perfume of every virtue,
the mirror of all purity.
You are joy in weeping, victory in battle,
and hope in death.

How sweet your name tastes in our mouth;
how harmoniously it rings in our ears;
what rapture it brings to our hearts!

You are the happiness of the suffering,
the crown of martyrs, the beauty of virgins.

We beg you guide us after this exile
to possession of your Son, Jesus. Amen.[42]

---

[42] John Paul II, Visit to the Marian Shrine of the Divine Love,
Rome, May 1, 1979.

We fly to thy protection

We fly to thy protection,
O Holy Mother of God;
Despise not our petitions
in our necessities,
but deliver us always from all dangers,
O glorious and blessed Virgin. Amen.

To St. Michael the Archangel

O glorious Prince of the heavenly host, St. Michael
the Archangel,
defend us in the battle and the terrible warfare
that we are waging against the principalities and
powers,
against the rulers of the world of darkness, against
the evil spirits.
Come to the aid of man,
whom Almighty God created immortal,
made in His own image and likeness,
and redeemed at a great price from the tyranny of
Satan.

The Church venerates thee as her protector and
patron.
To thee God has entrusted the souls of men to be
established in heavenly beatitude.

Oh, pray to the God of peace
that he may put Satan under our feet,

so far conquered that he may no longer be able
    to hold men in captivity and harm the Church.

Offer our prayers in the sight of the Most High,
so that they may quickly find mercy in the sight of
    the Lord.
And chaining the dragon, the ancient serpent, who
    is Satan, the Devil,
do thou again make him captive in the abyss,
that he may no longer seduce the nations. Amen.

Prayers for the Private Use of the Faithful Who Find Themselves Struggling Against the Powers of Darkness[43]

Have mercy on me, Lord, my God,
have mercy on me, Your servant:
a host of evil spirits ensnares me.
I am like a broken vessel.
Snatch me from the hands of my enemies.
Stay next to me; seek me if I am lost.
Bring me back to You after finding me and
do not abandon me after You have brought me
    back to You.
May I please You in all things,
knowing that You have redeemed me with Your
    mighty hands.
Through Christ our Lord. Amen.

[43] From Conferenza Episcopale Italiana, *Rito degli Esorcismi*, appendix II.

All powerful God,
You offer a home to refugees and
lead prisoners back to prosperity.
You see my affliction, and You come to
    my aid.
You defeat my mortal enemy,
so that, having fled his presence,
I may rediscover my liberty in peace
and, having returned to prayer
in serenity and tranquility,
I may proclaim how great You are
for having given victory to the people.
Through Christ our Lord. Amen.

O God, Creator and Protector of mankind,
You have created man in Your image
and, in a more admirable way,
You have recreated him through the grace
    of Baptism:
look upon me, Your servant, and hear my pleas:
may the splendor of Your glory rise in my heart,
and liberate me from every fear
and restore me to serenity of mind and spirit,
so that I may praise You and bless You
together with my brothers and sisters in the
    Church.
Through Christ our Lord. Amen.

God of mercy and source of every good,
You have wished that Your Son
submit to the torture of the Cross for us,

in order to liberate us from the power of our
   mortal enemy.
Look with kindness on my humiliation and my pain:
You who in the baptismal font
have made me a new creature,
help me to repel the assaults of the Evil One
and fill me with the grace of Your blessing.
Through Christ our Lord. Amen.

You have wished, O God,
to make me a child of the light through grace.
Do not permit the Evil One to cloak me in his
   darkness,
but permit me always to remain
in the radiant splendor of the liberty
that You have granted me,
through Christ our Lord. Amen.

Invocations to the Most Holy Trinity

Glory be to the Father, to the Son,
and to the Holy Spirit.
Glory and honor to God alone.

Let us bless the Father and the Son
with the Holy Spirit;
let us praise and exalt Him forever.

We invoke You,
we praise You,
and we adore You,
Holy Trinity.

You are our hope,
our salvation,
our glory,
O Blessed Trinity.

Liberate me,
save me,
renew my life,
O Blessed Trinity.

Holy, Holy, Holy Lord God almighty,
who was, who is, and who ever shall be.
To You, honor and power, O Blessed Trinity,
to You, glory and power forever.
To You, bestower of graces,
praise and glory forever and ever,
O Blessed Trinity.

Holy God,
Mighty God,
God Immortal,
have mercy on me.

Invocations to Christ the Lord

Jesus, Son of the living God, have mercy on me.
Jesus, image of the Father, have mercy on me.
Jesus, Eternal Wisdom, have mercy on me.
Jesus, splendor of eternal light, have mercy on me.
Jesus, Word of life, have mercy on me.
Jesus, Son of the Virgin Mary, have mercy on me.
Jesus, God and man, have mercy on me.
Jesus, High and Eternal Priest, have mercy on me.

Jesus, announcer of the Kingdom of God, have mercy
    on me.
Jesus, the way, the truth, and the life, have mercy on me.
Jesus, bread of life, have mercy on me.
Jesus, the true vine, have mercy on me.
Jesus, brother of the poor, have mercy on me.
Jesus, friend of sinners, have mercy on me.
Jesus, physician of souls and bodies, have mercy on me.
Jesus, salvation of the oppressed, have mercy on me.
Jesus, comforter of the wretched, have mercy on me.

You who have come into the world, have mercy on me.
You who have liberated the oppressed from the demon,
    have mercy on me.
You who hung on the Cross, have mercy on me.
You who accepted death for us, have mercy on me.
You who wished to lie in the tomb, have mercy on me.
You who descended into Hell, have mercy on me.
You who rose from the dead, have mercy on me.
You who ascended into Heaven, have mercy on me.
You who sent the Holy Spirit on the apostles, have mercy
    on me.
You who sit at the right hand of the Father, have mercy on
    me.
You who will come to judge the living and the dead, have
    mercy on me.

Through the mystery of your Incarnation, liberate me,
    Lord.
Through Your holy birth, liberate me, Lord.
Through Your holy baptism and fasting, liberate me, Lord.
Through Your Passion and Your Cross, liberate me, Lord

Through Your death and burial, liberate me, Lord.
Through Your holy Resurrection, liberate me, Lord.
Through Your glorious Ascension, liberate me, Lord.
Through the outpouring of the Holy Spirit, liberate me,
    Lord.
Through Your coming in glory, liberate me, Lord.

Each time the Cross is named, it is appropriate to make the Sign
    of the Cross.
Save me, O Christ redeemer, through the power of Your
    Cross:
You who saved Peter on the sea, have mercy on me.
By the holy Sign of the Cross,
liberate us, O Christ, from our enemies.
By Your holy Cross save us, O Christ redeemer,
You who in Your death have annihilated our death
and rising renewed our life.
We adore Your Cross, O Lord,
we venerate Your glorious Passion:
You who have suffered for us, have mercy on us.
We adore you, O Christ, and we bless you,
Because by Your holy Cross You have redeemed the world.

Invocations to the Blessed Virgin Mary
We fly to thy protection,
O holy Mother of God:
Despise not our petitions
in our necessities
but deliver us always
from all dangers,
O glorious and blessed Virgin,

Consoler of the afflicted, pray for us.
Help of Christians, pray for us.
Allow me to praise you, O holy Virgin.
Give me strength against your enemies.
My Mother, my trust,
Mary, Virgin Mother of God, pray to Jesus for me.
Mary, ever virgin, most honored queen of the world,
you gave birth to our Savior, Christ the Lord.
Intercede for our peace and our salvation.
Mary, Mother of grace and Mother of mercy,
protect us from the enemy and receive us
in the hour of our death.
Come to my assistance, most holy Virgin Mary,
in all my tribulations, distresses, and necessities:
ask your most beloved Son
to liberate me from every evil and danger
of soul and body.

The Memorare

Remember, O most gracious Virgin Mary
that never was it known
that anyone who fled to your protection,
implored your help or sought your intercession
was left unaided.
Inspired by this confidence I fly unto you,
O Virgin of virgins, my mother;
to you I come, before you I kneel,
sinful and sorrowful,
O Mother of the Word Incarnate,
despise not my petitions but in your mercy
hear and answer me. Amen.

Invocation to St. Michael the Archangel

St. Michael the Archangel, defend us in battle.
Be our defense against the
wickedness and snares of the Devil.
May God rebuke him, we humbly pray,
and do thou,
O Prince of the heavenly hosts,
by the power of God,
thrust into Hell Satan,
and all the evil spirits,
who prowl about the world
seeking the ruin of souls. Amen.

Litanies

Lord, have mercy, Lord, have mercy.
Christ, have mercy, Christ, have mercy.
Lord, have mercy, Lord, have mercy.
Holy Mary, Mother of God, pray for us [for me]
St. Michael, pray for us [for me].
St. Gabriel, pray for us [for me].
St. Raphael, pray for us [for me].
Holy Guardian Angels, pray for us [for me].
St. John the Baptist, pray for us [for me].
St. Joseph, pray for us [for me].
St. Peter, pray for us [for me].
St. Paul, pray for us [for me].
St. John the Evangelist, pray for us [for me].
Holy Apostles, pray for us [for me].
St. Mary Magdalene, pray for us [for me].
Other names of saints and the beatified can be added here.

From every sin, liberate us [liberate me], O Lord.

From the snares of the Devil, liberate us [liberate me], O Lord.

From eternal death, liberate us [liberate me], O Lord.

From every evil, liberate us [liberate me], O Lord.

Christ, hear us, [hear me] Christ, hear us, [hear me].

Christ graciously hear us [hear me], Christ graciously hear us [hear me].

Bibliography

Catechism of the Catholic Church. 2nd ed. Città del Vaticano: Libreria Editrice Vaticana, 1992.

Conferenza Episcopale Italiana. *Rito degli esorcismi e preghiere per circostanze particolari.* Città del Vaticano: Libreria Editrice Vaticana, 2001.

————. *Rito del battesimo.* Città del Vaticano: Libreria Editrice Vaticana, 2001.

Conferenza Episcopale Toscana. *A proposito di magia e di demonologia. Nota pastorale.* Città del Vaticano: Libreria Editrice Vaticana, 1994.

Congregazione per Il Culto Divino e la Disciplina Dei Sacramenti. *De exorcismis et supplicationibus quibusdam.* Città del Vaticano: Libreria Editrice Vaticana, 2001.

Denzinger, Heinrich. *Enchiridion Symbolorum.* Bologna: Edizioni Dehoniane, 1996.

Flannery, Austin, O.P., ed. *Vatican Council II, Constitutions, Decrees, Declarations.* Collegeville, MN: Liturgical Press, 1996.

Giuliani, Veronica. *Diario della vita interiore.* Translated by Leone Veuthey. Rome: Miscellanea Francescana, 2006.

Kowalska, Faustina. *Diario. La misericordia divina nella mia anima*. Città del Vaticano: Libreria Editrice Vaticana, 2014.

Pio XII. Titulus XII "De Exorcizandis Obsessis a Daemonio." In *Ritualis Romani*, Editio typica, 1952.

Thomas Aquinas, *Summa Theologica*.

Sophia Institute

Sophia Institute is a nonprofit institution that seeks to nurture the spiritual, moral, and cultural life of souls and to spread the Gospel of Christ in conformity with the authentic teachings of the Roman Catholic Church.

Sophia Institute Press fulfills this mission by offering translations, reprints, and new publications that afford readers a rich source of the enduring wisdom of mankind.

Sophia Institute also operates two popular online Catholic resources: CrisisMagazine.com and CatholicExchange.com.

Crisis Magazine provides insightful cultural analysis that arms readers with the arguments necessary for navigating the ideological and theological minefields of the day. *Catholic Exchange* provides world news from a Catholic perspective as well as daily devotionals and articles that will help you to grow in holiness and live a life consistent with the teachings of the Church.

In 2013, Sophia Institute launched Sophia Institute for Teachers to renew and rebuild Catholic culture through service to Catholic education. With the goal of nurturing the spiritual, moral, and cultural life of souls, and an abiding respect for the role and work of teachers, we strive to provide materials and programs that are at once enlightening to the mind and ennobling to the heart; faithful and complete, as well as useful and practical.

Sophia Institute gratefully recognizes the Solidarity Association for preserving and encouraging the growth of our apostolate over the course of many years. Without their generous and timely support, this book would not be in your hands.

www.SophiaInstitute.com
www.CatholicExchange.com
www.CrisisMagazine.com
www.SophiaInstituteforTeachers.org

Sophia Institute Press® is a registered trademark of Sophia Institute.
Sophia Institute is a tax-exempt institution as defined by the
Internal Revenue Code, Section 501(c)(3). Tax I.D. 22-2548708.